"The study of populism as a communicative phenomenon is vitally important in current times. Elena Block has made a highly valuable contribution to this field, identifying discursive commonalities in the otherwise very different political projects of Hugo Chavez and Donald Trump. This book will be keenly sought after by those studying populism as a media as well as a political phenomenon."

Terry Flew, *Professor of Digital Communications and Culture, The University of Sydney*

"Populism in its various shapes is undoubtedly a key feature of contemporary politics around the globe. When looking at the threats it poses to democracy, left-wing or right-wing authoritarian leaders show no difference: they share contempt for democratic institutions and use divisive language. This timely book provides insights on the callous communication strategies of such leaders as Trump and Chávez, reflecting on the ethical dimension of populist language and on what the author aptly terms "discursive disruption" of populism of the 21st century.

Gianpietro Mazzoleni, *The University of Milan*

"In Populist Communication and Democracy: The Cases of Hugo Chávez and Donald J. Trump, Elena Block creates the concept of discursive disruption in order to explain how, from opposing ideologies, these leaders used their populist style to divide their audiences to the detriment of republican values. With incivility and intolerance, and this linguistic weapon, populists win the quasi-religious loyalty of their followers. Discursive disruption is a powerful framework for analysis. This book is worth considering and using for future studies."

Alexandra Alvarez, *Universidad de Los Andes (ULA)*

Discursive Disruption, Populist Communication and Democracy: The Cases of Hugo Chávez and Donald J. Trump

In *Discursive Disruption, Populist Communication and Democracy: The Cases of Hugo Chávez and Donald J. Trump*, Elena Block explores the links between declining democratic discourses and populist communication, and reflects on the communicative and moral dimensions of populism.

Block proposes the concept of discursive disruption to help to identify, analyze, and understand the disruptive power of populist speech, turning to the communicative styles of Venezuela's late President Hugo Chávez and the US's President Donald J. Trump to illustrate and support this new conceptual and analytical tool. While the mainstream political class and media traditionally sought to manage the processes of political communication, the book contends that they have now been displaced and their role has been undermined. Middle ground politics and journalism have been substituted by the adversarial rhetorical styles of populists, multiplied through multi-fragmented channels, texts, and voices. With this book, Block continues her introspection in the conceptual, communicative, and mediatic dimensions of populism by adding a perspective that draws on democratic and discursive theories.

Discursive Disruption, Populist Communication and Democracy: The Cases of Hugo Chávez and Donald J. Trump is ideally designed for scholars and professional communicators in political science and communication studies eager to understand the connection between weakening discourses of modern democracy and the pervasiveness of confrontational styles of populist communication in contemporary political exchanges.

Elena Block is Lecturer in Strategic Communication at the School of Communication and Arts at the University of Queensland. She holds a PhD in Political Communication from The University of Queensland

and MSc in Political Sociology from the London School of Economic and Political Science (LSE). Her main areas of interest: political communication; strategic communication; populist communication; the mediatisation of politics and society; virtual and teen influencers; and their role and impact on strategic communication and advocacy.

Routledge Research in Political Communication

For more information about this series, please visit: https://www.routledge.com/Routledge-Research-in-Political-Communication/book-series/PC

1   **The Media, Political Participation and Empowerment**
    Edited by Richard Scullion, Roman Gerodimos, Daniel Jackson and Darren Lilleker

2   **Digital World: Connectivity, Creativity and Rights**
    Edited by Gillian Youngs

3   **Political Marketing**
    Strategic 'Campaign Culture'
    Edited by Kostas Gouliamos, Antonis Theocharous, Bruce Newman, Stephan Henneberg

4   **Politics and the Internet in Comparative Context**
    Views from the cloud
    Edited by Paul G. Nixon, Rajash Rawal and Dan Mercea

5   **Political Communication Online**
    Structures, Functions, and Challenges
    Ognyan Seizov

6   **Political Communication in the Online World**
    Theoretical Approaches and Research Designs
    Edited by Gerhard Vowe and Philipp Henn

7   **Discursive Disruption, Populist Communication and Democracy**
    The Cases of Hugo Chávez and Donald J. Trump
    Elena Block

Discursive Disruption, Populist Communication and Democracy

The Cases of Hugo Chávez and Donald J. Trump

Elena Block

NEW YORK AND LONDON

Cover image: Focus Template Cover

First published 2022
by Routledge
605 Third Avenue, New York, NY 10158

and by Routledge
4 Park Square, Milton Park, Abingdon, Oxon, OX14 4RN

*Routledge is an imprint of the Taylor & Francis Group, an
informa business*

Library of Congress Cataloging-in-Publication Data
A catalog record for this title has been requested

ISBN: 978-0-367-62619-8 (hbk)
ISBN: 978-0-367-63276-2 (pbk)
ISBN: 978-1-003-11860-2 (ebk)

DOI: 10.4324/9781003118602

Typeset in Times New Roman
by KnowledgeWorks Global Ltd.

To Dr. Elenita and John.

To Tatiana, nieces and nephews in Venezuela and scattered across two continents.

To Aura, Carmen Elena, and Mery.

To the 5.6 (and growing) million Venezuelan migrants.

Contents

List of Illustrations   xiii
Acknowledgments   xiv

1 The disruption is discursive   1

  1.1   *The rise of populist rhetoric 3*
  1.2   *Disrupted impressions of democracy 6*
  1.3   *Blame it on* language *8*
  1.4   *Babel as a metaphor 10*
  1.5   Trumping *discursive and communicative democracy 13*
  1.6   *From the abusive populist talk to* political communication shutdowns *14*
  1.7   *Aims and structure 16*
       References 17

2 Democracy, trust, truths, lies…and style   21

  2.1   *Trust, truths, and lies in politics 22*
  2.2   *The eroded discourses of democracy 26*
  2.3   *Populism versus democracy 32*
  2.4   *Critical political communication, style, and discursive violence 34*
       References 37

3 Populist communication, discursive violence, and disrupted democracy   42

  3.1   *Authoritarian populist communication 42*
  3.2   *Western democratic discourses 51*

3.3   *Discursive disruption 60*
       References 62

4 The discursive disruption framework   68

4.1   *Pilot study: The Chávez-Trump déjà vu 69*
4.2   *Approach to the analysis and method 72*
4.3   *The discursive disruption analytical framework 74*
       References 79

5 Chávez and Trump as paradigms of discursive disruption   81

5.1   *Use of language 81*
5.2   *Construction of identity 88*
5.3   *Use of and relationship with the media 92*
5.4   *Adherence or not to traditional democratic discourses 97*
       References 103

6 The moral language of populist communication   109

6.1   *The discursive ethos of populist power 110*
6.2   *The moral language of political*
       communication, Chávez and Trump 120
       References 125

Index   129

List of figures

1.1 'POPULISMS' (2019). Courtesy of Visual Artist Sean
    Mackaoui   8
1.2 Cildo Meireles' "Babel 2001"   12
3.1 "Populism for Dummies" (2016). Courtesy of visual
    artist Eduardo Sanabria, EDO Ilustrado   46
4.1 Similarities (S) and Differences (D) Chávez-Trump
    2015–2019   70
4.2 Heatmap: Topics of Similarities and Differences Between
    Chávez-Trump 2015–2019   71
4.3 Discursive Disruption Analytical Framework:
    Key Variables   76
5.1 *Amor en tiempos de Trump* (2017). Courtesy of
    visual artist Rayma Suprani   86
6.1 Discursive Disruption Indicators and Implications Frame 119

Acknowledgments

I am deeply grateful to Emeritus Professor Ralph Negrine for his support, patience, and insights, especially at the early stages of this book. To Vivienne Chávez for helping me proofread, edit, and give coherence to the manuscript. To Venezuelan visual artists Rayma Suprani and EDO (Eduardo Sanabria) for allowing me to use their brilliant works; also, to European artist Sean Mackaoui, and Brazilian contemporary artist Cildo Meireles, the Tate Gallery, and Gallerie Lelong & Co., who kindly gave their permission to use their excellent pieces to illustrate this book. To Stephan Guillou for his invaluable help with R GGpLot visualizations. To Evangelene Dickson for kindly coming to my rescue to resize tables and graphs. To my reviewers, who with their critique, comments and recommendations helped me improve my initial, rather clumsy, text. To Routledge's senior editor Natalja Mortensen and assistant editor Charlie Baker, for their patience, kind support, and, especially for understanding, the long time it took me to finish this book written in times of COVID-19. To all of them my everlasting gratitude, respect, and admiration.

1 The disruption is discursive

Amid the topics that have dominated the political communication agenda in the first two decades of the 21st century, I have been particularly absorbed by two: Rising populist rhetoric and disrupted and weakening discourses of democracy. Is there a connection between these two themes? Of what nature? This book argues that among the many disruptions experienced by humans in contemporary democratic societies, there is a fundamental one of a *discursive* nature, which I call *discursive disruption*. I propose discursive disruption not only as a process, but also as a conceptual and analytical tool that serves to identify, analyze, and make sense of disruptive communication strategies and speech styles with the power to transgress, upset, and even change the discourses and conventions of democracy. At the heart of discursive disruption, I argue, there is an antidialogic/ monologic – and hence *antidemocratic* – speech style that has typically characterized populist actors in positions of power.

I understand antidialogic/monologic political communication following Freire (1970) and Bakhtin (1981) as a type of communication that is authoritarian, one-sided, emotional, and intolerant that has become normalized and has at moments, and in some actual or virtual environments, prevailed over plural and civil democratic interactions. In this book, I assess whether such antidialogic communicative practices have led to disruptions and even shutdowns of the political dialogue in some democratic, or formerly democratic, countries.

This book explores disruptive and antidialogic political practices from the perspective of communicative power, defined by Hepp (2013) as the implementation of an individual or group's will "through communication" (p. 62). The discursive disruption framework advanced by this book serves to analyze the use of a communicative kind of power that enables its wielders to mobilize antagonistic, prejudiced, and often irrational arguments about

DOI: 10.4324/9781003118602-1

democracy through *symbolic* means (words, texts, signs, visuals, channels, platforms). Frankfurt School social psychologist Erich Fromm (2013) explained that symbolic language is driven by a "different logic" that is governed by our senses and emotions rather than rationality, and where "intensity and association" (p. 13) rule instead of time or space. The mixed use of communicative power and symbolic language suggests an irrational type of political communication which, for Fitzduff (2017), appeals to individuals or groups who prefer leaders that "speak with certainty" (p. 9) about issues that concern them, no matter if their claims lack logic or are not true. These types of politicians appeal because they give people hope through distorted or fallacious imaginaries housed in alternate realities. Such Panglossian and fallacious approach to politics may explain why rational, cautious and at times hesitant consensus-seeking leaders are often unpopular among audiences who do not care about rational or sedate politics. Furthermore, I am referring here to contemporary political leaders who are savvy in the use of words, media, and identity discourses with the aim to "interrupt the flow of communication" (Anthony, 2021) in the construction of power. Digital strategist Bosco Anthony (2021) argued in one of my Master of Communication seminars, at the University of Queensland, that we are at a critical age when information is so pervasive that communicative disruption (or *discursive disruption*, as I call it) has become necessary to capture our audience's attention. While populist politicians appear to be sagacious disruptors, mainstream politicians seem to favor formal, sober, calmer paths to deal with political issues.

In sum, this study is, above all, a theoretical inquiry that uses two salient case studies to illustrate and support its reflections on discursive disruption. I review the political communication styles of two controversial populist leaders, Venezuela's late President Hugo Chávez and the United States' (US) President Donald Trump, who despite their significant ideological, cultural, and socioeconomic differences are emblematic of the antidialogic/monologic, rather antidemocratic, political communication style interrogated in this book. This investigation reflects my scholarly concern about the power of populist speech and its disruptive impact on contemporary democracies.

To develop the discursive disruption framework and the two case studies, I pursue three lines of inquiry: First, I critically review contemporary political communication events that have been represented as disruptive to democracy in the academic literature, news media articles, recognized public opinion investigations or surveys, and political speeches; second, I develop a theoretical reflection through which I assess and link existing theories and conceptual premises to build the discursive disruption frame, which can help to get a better understanding of democratic disruptions that are often linked with populism. Finally, I analyze the two case studies by testing Venezuela's Chávez's and the US's Trump's speech performances through my proposed discursive disruption frame. Hence, in this book, I continue my introspection in the conceptual, communicative, and mediatic dimensions of populism, developed in previous work (see Block, 2015; Block & Negrine, 2017) by adding a perspective that draws on democratic and discursive theories to offer a new conceptual and analytical frame.

1.1 The rise of populist rhetoric

After situating this book's argument and lines of inquiry, I will now put them in context: A linage of authoritarian populist actors, until now typical of autocratic, antipolitical, outspoken, and personalized Latin American caudillos, has been advancing electorally across several Western democratic countries. While the mainstream political class and media traditionally sought to manage the processes of political communication, they have now been displaced and their role has been severely undermined. Middle-ground politics and journalism have been increasingly substituted by adversarial rhetorical discourses that are typical of media-savvy populists of the right and left, algorithmically amplified through multifragmented channels, texts, and voices. Extreme positions and blunt intolerance toward those who think differently have not only become widespread and normalized but celebrated in both face-to-face and social media political interactions.

Conventional, center-ground, non-extremist, democratic discourses are viewed with suspicion, contempt, or both. An investigative piece, sponsored by *The Guardian* (Lewis et al., 2019), which analyzed speeches from 140 political leaders in 40 countries, suggested that the divisive populist rhetoric has had a surge in the last 20 years. The research, undertaken by a group of academics led by Professor Kirk Hawkins, claimed that the populist rhetoric average doubled from the early 2000s, when it was 0.2, to late 2019, when it rose to 0.4. The research suggested that "politicians across the globe have gradually adopted more populist arguments, framing politics as a Manichean battle between the will of ordinary people and corrupt, self-serving elites" (Lewis et al., 2019, para. 3), a claim that is consistent with

Hawkins's (2010) earlier research on Chávez's Manichean populist discourse. Notably, *The Guardian's* study represented Chávez as "the most populist leader of their database" (Lewis et al., 2019, para. 7); the same study also found that the worldwide rise of populist leaders to prime ministerial and presidential positions, such as Donald Trump in the US, "transformed the terms of the debate" (para. 8) in their respective countries.

Moreover, there is an emerging body of research that suggests that polarized political communication often matches equally polarized news audiences. For example, Hameleers's (2019a; 2019b) studies on populist audiences have indicated a correlation between the language used by populist leaders, partisan media, and online news audiences. More specifically, Hameleers's (2019a) study of online news in the US, United Kingdom (UK), and The Netherlands indicated that news audiences "respond to partisan news with congruent polarized interpretations" (p. 485). Fletcher et al.'s (2020) research about online and offline news audiences in 12 countries (US, UK, and 10 European countries) found higher levels of polarization in the US', UK's, and pluralist/southern countries' online audiences than in democratic corporatist countries, where there is less news media fragmentation. Fletcher et al. (2020) particularly suggested that there is a need for more audience-centric polarization studies that exceed left-right categorizations, a claim that is consistent with one of the arguments that I develop in this study: Populist communication research needs to go beyond binary classifications mainly based on ideology. Populist actors use ideology at whim, as a discursive tool in the construction of power; for example, the way Trump called Biden a "radical socialist" to appeal to Hispanic anticommunist communities in Florida; or the way Chávez used to call his opponents, "imperialists", or "empire cubs".

Populism involves a political communication style, a set of communicative strategies and devices that are used in the construction of power and identity to appeal to politically disenchanted or alienated audiences. Although contemporary populist actors savvily use democratic means and the media to be elected, once in power and over time they tend to overly criticize, decry, and disparage democratic language and conventions. Although there is an increasing body of research on populist communication and populist rhetoric, a mixed study of populist communication and the rejection or contempt that populist leaders often express for democracy remains less interrogated. This is the main gap I am trying to address with this book's reflections on discursive disruption.

It has become commonplace to hear that we are living in times of disruption as the discourses that have underpinned democracy since the end of World War II and the Cold War are under pressure. The literature on disruption has diversified since French (1941) wrote a psychological study about group disruption and cohesion, explaining how differing views among group members triggered frustrations that led to divisions. The last two decades have been prolific in multidisciplinary approaches to disruption, from Fukuyama's (2000) political economy book on what he called "The great disruption"; Schmidt and Cohen's (2010) article on "Digital Disruption"; and Vollmer's (2013) sociological study on disruption, disaster, and social change, to more recent pieces by de Waal (2018), Stiegler (2019), and Krastev (2014) concerned with disruptions in the fields of "civil leadership", "computational capitalism", and "global protests", respectively.

In this context, this book specifically focuses on the links between populist communication and disruptions of democratic discourses. By analyzing Chavez and Trump, two very different and highly controversial populist presidents who were democratically elected, I am aware that I am studying two topical characters that have disrupted and even changed the political conversation in their respective countries; two leaders who, however, have been little analyzed *together* from a critical communication perspective. In my study, I review how Chávez's inflammatory rhetoric was one of the main triggering factors leading to his country's endemic divisions, constant violence, and a long lasting autocratic regime that transformed Venezuela into a failed state; also, how Trump's incendiary rhetoric fueled ongoing public controversy (pre, during and after his presidency), violent clashes between extreme groups, and, especially, the Capitol Hill insurrection that contributed to make him the first President impeached twice in American history. At the heart of these events is a discourse, a communication style that begs for deeper and reflective evaluation. As Davis (2019) argued, contested democratic conventions call for political communication scholars to ask "difficult questions" about their validity, but also, I suggest, about the origin, causes, and validity of the contestation itself.

Diverse think tanks and public opinion research centers have been monitoring weakening trends of democracy in the last decade. For example, Freedom House's (2019) report, entitled "Democracy in

Retreat", indicated a decline in democratic indicators, such as political rights and civil liberties.

Eisen et al.'s (2019) report published by the Brookings Institution on the state of democracy added a relevant element: The rise of "autocracy" within democracy at a global level suggests that "the world has entered a new wave of autocratization" (p. 8).

Apropos the Cambridge Analytica scandal and Donald Trump's 2016 presidential election, the UK's Information Commissioner's Office (ICO; 2018), the independent body that "upholds information rights in the public interest" (para. 1), published a report entitled "Democracy disrupted?", which discussed the impact of data analytics and micro targeting on political campaigning. One of the ICO's (2018) significant findings is that there is a concerning lack of transparency and "provision of fair processing information" (p. 3) about how social media platforms (particularly Facebook) use citizens' personal data and the way they are targeted by political campaigns. I will expand my review on think tank studies about weakening democracy in Chapter 2.

The foregoing discussion confirms two fundamental issues: Populist rhetoric is rising, and democratic discourses have been weakening or "disrupted"; hence, the main question I ask in this book: Are there any connections between the two?

1.2 Disrupted impressions of democracy

Erving Goffman (1959) anticipated six decades ago that "impressions fostered in everyday performances are subject to disruption" (p. 66), suggesting that the steps to follow would be to find out which kinds of "impressions" would have the power to "shatter" accepted or normalized constructions of reality. Thus, drawing on Goffman (1959), I explore the links between disruptions in "fostered" discourses of modern Western democracy and the communicative strategies and styles enacted by populist players in some democratic or formerly democratic countries. I argue that the antidialogic/monologic communication strategies used by populist leaders in positions of power have played a role in shattering the discourses, norms of interaction, or conventions of democracy that prevailed in their countries before they came to power. I am talking about democratic discourses that had been traditionally, and broadly, rooted in principles and values associated with modern democracy, namely, freedoms (of speech, information, association, belief, religion, peaceful protest), civil rights, social justice, rule of law, separation of power, and plural and rational deliberation in society.

One additional, more specific question has been fundamental to the argument proposed by this book: What kind of political communication strategies have had the power to disrupt, or "shatter" fostered discourses and conventions of modern democracy?

To seek answers to my questions, I take a critical communication approach centered on studying issues of power, communication, and identity, with a special focus on the use of language, style, and the role of media. Despite significant ideological, sociopolitical, and cultural arguments against studying them together (Gill, 2016; Harris, 2018), my two case studies, Chávez and Trump, share fundamental stylistic traits in the way they have used communication and media (see Bolivar, 2018; de la Torre, 2017), which makes them typical cases of the phenomenon I explore in this book.

This explains why I argue that populism is more about *communication* and *style* than ideology. Populist communication is about how populist politicians use antipolitical and emotional communication strategies that are attractive to politically disenchanted citizens. For example, Rooduijn and Akkerman's (2017) study of 32 political parties in Western European countries suggested that both left and right radical parties "are inclined to employ a populist discourse" (p. 193). Political communication scholarship has further demonstrated this point: Mazzoleni and Bracciale (2018) found common features in the way right and left, "soft" and "bold", populists communicate and use the media in Italy. This is consistent with Ernst et al.'s (2019) study on how 31 European populist parties use social media, where they found that although populism of the right and left "differ in their ideologies, party programs, and social basis" (p. 6), they share important traits that are all related to the use of communication.

Putting aside their politics or ideologies, populist leaders, such as Chávez and Trump, have decried the language and conventions of plural deliberation and coexistence in a democratic society; both are bothered by or wary of the separation of powers and accountability, and both have been intolerant of news media's criticism.

Therefore, discursive disruption as a process, and especially as a conceptual frame, can assist to recognize, anticipate, and face, if necessary, the challenges posed by the language of contemporary populist communicators. As an anecdotal illustration, Figure 1.1 shows a collage cartoon called "Populisms", by visual artist Sean Mackaoui (2019), which evokes the Aristotle and Plato detail from the *School of Athens* fresco in the Vatican collection. The faces of some of the most disruptive 21st-century populist leaders can be identified in the cartoon, Trump and Chávez amongst them.

Figure 1.1 'POPULISMS' (2019). Courtesy of Visual Artist Sean Mackaoui. The faces of notorious populist leaders of our times can be spotted here, from Trump, Chávez, Johnson, and Bolsonaro, to Salvini, Kirchner, Duterte, and Erdoğan.

1.3 Blame it on *language*

From different perspectives, Vox's founder and editor-at-large, Ezra Klein (2020), and political scientist and economist, Francis Fukuyama (2020), have stressed the role of polarization as the "greatest weakness" of Western, specifically American, democracy. Klein (2020) blamed polarization on racial issues and identity politics. Fukuyama (2020) agreed but added that identity exceeds race. Fukuyama (2020) argued that politicians need to take into account the "moral appeal" that national identity exerts on people and recommended liberal politicians to show more "empathy for the legitimate concerns of a working class that is in serious trouble" (para. 16). These arguments show the importance of studying the populist manipulation of identity politics in power relations. For example, the way Trump used Black Lives Matter protests as a counter argument to the Capitol Hill insurrection. Or the way Chávez continued to represent himself as an antielite political outsider, even after being in the Presidency – and hence the head of the new political elite – for 13 years (Block, 2015).

The construction of identity requires extreme and abrasive kind of language. Using a phrase that has become a sort of cliché today (but does not make it less true), speech matters, words matter: At the heart of today's democratic dysfunctions and disruptions is language, the way some political and media actors and citizens – mainly the populist – use words to interact in politics and name (and shame) people and political things. Hence, the title of this chapter: democratic disruptions are originally *discursive*, as such disruptions involve speech acts and idiosyncratic communication styles.

The decline of political language has been addressed before from different perspectives, both in editorial pieces and in academic articles and books, some of which initially inspired my investigation about the topic. For example, *The New York Times*'s CEO and former *BBC* director general Mark Thompson (2016) argued in an article published by *The Guardian*, that historically, failures in democracy, human freedoms and rights, as well as the rise of tyrannies and totalitarianism have been associated with "a breakdown in public language" (para. 1). Thompson (2017) later published a book where he suggested that political rhetoric has become "stale", which has led to mistrust in politics and the media and to voters' preference for the "authenticity" promised by populists. However, despite actively working in the editorial world, he does not link declining political language with communication or media issues, as he seems to consider political language as the sole factor for democratic failure. Political language, however, does not act on its own or in a void, as it is part of a political communication interaction, and a context, where words, but also culture, power, media, and identity matter.

Intellectual historians Ball et al. (1989) explained three decades ago, "Many of the major works of political philosophy can be read as responses to, reflections upon, and antidotes for conceptual chaos and communicative breakdown" (p. 2). They argued that building conceptual histories can widen "the unidimensional discourse" (p. 4) that has characterized the political conversations in the West, or Western-influenced countries. This argument suggests that in the light of 21st-century disruptions, the discourses that have characterized democracy need to be retraced, discussed, and rethought to have a more comprehensive and critical perspective of contemporary events.

For example, in a darker piece about digital disruption, Stiegler (2019) wrote about new forms of "barbarism" brought by digitalization and "algorithmic governmentality" to democratic societies. Conversely, from a linguistics perspective, Archibugi (2005) claimed that "democratic politics should imply the willingness of all players to make an effort to understand each other…to overcome the barriers to mutual understanding, particularly the linguistic ones" (p. 537). Indeed, democratic politics should be about listening to each other, and recognizing and respecting each other's views both physically and digitally. However, today we live in an era where being intolerant toward those who think differently has become the norm, even trendy.

1.4 Babel as a metaphor

The last decade of the 20th century and the first two decades of the millennium have seen how shared spaces for plural deliberation are not only thinning but are also viewed with cynicism, as useless or corrupt spaces for politicking. As an example, just see how notorious post-millennial environmental activist, Greta Thunberg, pejoratively and repeatedly represents political leaders' summits as pure "blah, blah, blah" (BBC News, 2021). Twenty-first century political communication has turned into a world of one-sided antidialogic interactions (Freire, 1970), and monologic utterances that assume "passive listeners" (Bakhtin, 1981) are willing to agree to extreme and emotional positions regardless of whether they are validated by facts or logic. This panorama reflects assertive or fanatical arguments where rumors and facts, fake and reality continuously blur. In his *Limited Inc* writings, Bakhtin (1981) argued that in the democratic world, particularly in the US and Europe, philosophers, theoreticians, and ideologists promoting "the classical ethics of proof, discussion and exchange" (p. 157) are the same ones that often fail to read and listen to others, demonstrate dogmatism, and mix "science and chatter" as if they are afraid of communication. It is a world where the confounding languages of the biblical Babel reign.

The Babelian myth has had various interpretations and representations across history and scholarly fields. The book of Genesis (Ignatius Press, 2009, 11: 1–9) tells the story of the ambitious people that inhabited the "whole earth", people that had a single and uncomplicated language. Although these biblical people decided to build a tower to heaven to make "a name for themselves" (11: 6), their God thought that humanity exceeded the idea of a single people and language and thereupon "confused" and "scattered them abroad" (11: 8), a divine action and metaphor that might be interpreted as the beginning of a multicultural world. Baktkin (1981), for example, saw Babel as a positive metaphor, as an artistic and dialectic "maypole" around which a multiplicity of languages, and, hence, the possibility of dialogue emerged. Hiebert (2007), from a biblical literature perspective, represented Babel as a sort of divine gift that boosted and celebrated diversity by setting free different cultures and languages against the Babelian monologic aspirations.

Other scholars have interpreted the Babelian myth in a different light, focusing on the Babelian confusion and the importance of building a common civic language. Intellectual historians grouped in Ball et al. (1989) approached Babel ethically, cautioning against cases of "communicative entropy" that could lead to "individual isolation and mute violence" (p. 1); these scholars stressed the importance of a moral or political language that could become "a medium of shared understanding" (p. 1) between different groups, which should not be reduced to the single natural language that the Babelian biblical inhabitants aimed. The loss of a shared *ethical* language, understood as the language of democracy or the res publica, would lead to "the loss of community and the destruction of a common world" (Ball et al., 1989, p. 1). One wonders then whether the political world has lost, or perhaps never had, a shared *minimum political moral language*, a civic, *human* language, that could serve to communicate *politically* with and among different peoples despite cultural and linguistic diversities.

Political communication scholars, Brants and Voltmer (2011), also saw Babel as a challenge for post-democratic societies; they used the Babel metaphor to explain how continuously changing communication technologies were turning political communication into "grey noise of meaningless and disjointed messages nobody is listening to" (p. 1). Thus, the Babel metaphor has been given a rather paradoxical representation in the literature as both the multiplication of languages and communicative confusion and closure. Contemporary mediatized and datafied democratic societies exhibit extreme and rather clannish communicative interactions. Politically engaged and connected citizens mainly listen to the sound of their own voices and the voices of the likeminded, a process exacerbated by intense, emotional, often ephemeral and superficial social media interactions.

The last two discussions above conjure or evoke artistic representations of Babelian communicative confusion. For example, Cildo Meireles' (2001) installation "Babel 2001" at the Tate Gallery is a visionary piece made of vintage analogue radios, all playing at once, which embodies a world of ongoing mediatized talk and noise where nobody really *communicates* (see Figure 1.2). "Babel 2001" suggests that sophisticated technology and multiple and simultaneous talks do not necessarily guarantee a communicative society where individuals and groups have a voice, listen to, and recognize each other; one may listen to everybody and nobody at the same time.

Figure 1.2 Cildo Meireles' "Babel 2001"

Source: Photo authorized by the Tate Gallery – © Cildo Meireles Courtesy Galerie Lelong & Co., New York

1.5 *Trumping* discursive and communicative democracy

Russell L. Hanson (1989) argued three decades ago, in an essay about changes in the concept of democracy, that we have been used to living in a world that agreed "on the importance and desirability of democracy" (p. 68). In 1951, UNESCO highlighted the acceptance of the democratic ideal as "the highest form of political or social organization" (McKeon, 1951, as cited in Hanson, 1989, p. 68). However, the certainty about the virtues of modern democracy wobbled in the 1960s when the concept began to lose its association with the significant socioeconomic, cultural, and political problems, and structures that had quintessentially shaped the idea and meaning of democracy.

I use the term modern or conventional democracy to describe dominant discourses of democracy in the last century, a topic that I develop in Chapter 3. Democracy has been represented differently depending on scholarly classifications or types (see, e.g., Farrelly, 2015; Norris, 2008; Pateman, 1970). Specifically, Farrelly (2015) identified the following categories: (a) liberal or "legal", (b) representative (either "competitive elitist" or "classic pluralist"), and (c) participatory, deliberative or "discursive" democracy. The concept of discursive democracy proposed by critical thinker John Dryzek (2002) is relevant to my argument. He defined discursive democracy as pluralistic spaces for "contestation of discourses" (p. 163), where citizens can communicate across difference and reflect "upon preferences in a non-coercive fashion" (p. 163). Dryzek's, and also Iris Young's (1997), approaches to deliberative, or *communicative*, democracy are viewed as radical paradigms of democratic deliberation (Walter, 2008). As Farrelly (2015) noted, the final decade of the 20th century produced what was called the "deliberative turn", which suggested that at the heart of democracy, its discourses, conventions or rules of interaction are, or should be, free, plural, and reflective forms of deliberation and contestation among citizens (in contrast with the well-meant but idealistic Habermasian quest for consensus).

In the 1990s, Young (1997a) proposed "communicative democracy" as an ideal form of democracy. She stressed:

> when political dialogue aims at solving collective problems, it justly requires a plurality of perspectives, speaking styles, and ways of expressing the particularity of [a] social situation as well as the general applicability of principles.
>
> (p. 73)

Iris Young (1997b) stressed the importance of plural deliberation contrasting "the politics of difference" against "identity politics" (p. 383). She proposed the politics of difference as the practice that facilitates individuals and groups to fight political and social unfairness and imbalances within a democracy. The politics of difference is the opposite of identity politics. For Young (1997b), identity politics is the discourse to blame when "democracy falters" as *blind loyalty* to identity groups has led to a "retribalization" of politics, to a *clannish* type of politics. She argued that identity politics is a toxic exclusive practice through which "any possibility for human dialogue, for democratic communication and commonality, vanishes as so much froth on the polluted sea of phony equality" (p. 384). This argument suggests that communication is the ethos of democracy. Democracy *is* communication.

Therefore, in this book, I propose the concept of discursive disruption as directly opposite to discursive, deliberative, and, especially, communicative democracy. Discursive disruption is a process but also a framework that serves to understand whether and how the antidialogic/monologic, arrogant and abrasive, identity-driven communication strategies of populist players trump the discourses and conventions of democracy. When plural and democratic communication and dialogue are interrupted, shattered to the point of closure or shutdown, I suggest, we are in the presence of discursive disruption.

1.6 From the abusive populist talk to *political communication shutdowns*

The last claim that I aim to demonstrate in this book is that the popularization and normalization of the antidialogic/monologic styles might eventually lead to *political communication shutdowns*. For example, legal and constitutional changes and amendments boosted by Hugo Chávez gradually turned Venezuela into a long-lasting populist autocracy, where separation of power, independent judiciary, respect for human rights, civil liberties and rule of law, transparent elections, and, above all, *rational* and mutually respectful dialogue between parties or groups have been impossible for over two decades. The United Nations Human Rights (2019) report on Venezuela noted the following: "as of 31 May 2019, 793 people remain arbitrarily deprived of their liberty, including 58 women, and that so far this year, 22 deputies of the National Assembly, including its President, have been stripped of their parliamentary immunity" (para. 11).

I am not suggesting that this situation is solely due to chavismo's populist discourses. Complex political economy developments that have transformed Venezuela from a booming oil country to a failed state, increasing struggles over power (between and within government and divided and weak opposition groups), the actions of rogue and violent groups often associated with chavismo (which involve guerrilla, drug trafficking and illegal mining gangs), and the ongoing exacerbation of identity politics are some of the main elements that have played important roles in Venezuela's state of affairs. However, I argue that the divisive, insulting, skillfully mediatized identity discourses of *Chavismo* have played a leading role in the current situation.

In regard to Trump's discourse and daily tirades, a *Washington Post's* investigation of 28,000 cases of bullying in schools in the US suggested that the president's "inflammatory language", "has seeped to schools across America...with kids mimicking the president's insults and the cruel way he delivers them" (Tharoor, 2020, para. 8). In addition, Trump's verbal disdain for the rule of law (Biskupic, 2020) is a topic of concern. It is now commonsense to talk about Trump's incendiary speeches that boosted the January 6, 2021 Capitol Hill uprising that led to his second impeachment. Incendiary language for which he was not only unrepentant but proud (Petri, 2021).

In the early 21st century, informed citizens have witnessed how arguably successful communication strategies used by populist players, such as Trump in the US or Chávez in Venezuela, have taken traditional politics and journalism by surprise and unpreparedness. It seems as if elite and legacy politics and media have not realized that times, situations, and practices have become unpopular or turned irrelevant since the times when, as Yasha Mounk (2018) put it, "despite deep disagreements" (p. 18), all major political actors were willing to play by the rules of the democratic game. Therefore, the study of populist communication and its links with declining democratic discourses matters because, in this unpreparedness, the fabric of democracy has progressively been disrupted, eroded, and in some cases, such as in Venezuela, destroyed.

Authoritarian populists leaders, such as Donald Trump in the US and Hugo Chávez in Venezuela, have tended to use democracy to get elected, but their words and subsequent actions express distrust or even contempt for politics and democracy. Populist leaders tend to bypass democratic speech conventions or norms of interaction, and in some cases, the constitutions of their countries. This happened in embattled chavista Venezuela when after his attempted 1992 coup, Chávez said to his loyalists: "Comrades, regretfully, for now, our objectives were not achieved" (Chávez, 1992). After the coup, Chávez went to prison for two years, was pardoned, actively campaigned within democracy, and won the 1998 presidential election. After his victory, and boosted by his popularity, Chávez promoted a change of constitution, the same constitution through which he was first elected and that he deemed as "moribund" during his first, rather bizarre and offensive for many, swearing-in ceremony. After 21 years of chavismo, Venezuela is considered a "collapsed country" or "failed state" (Hausmann, 2017; Naim & Toro, 2018).

In the US, Trump's "bizarro" interpretations of the impeachment proceedings, mainly verbalized through Twitter posts or *Fox News*, intended to place him "above the law", as Georgetown University law professor and former Obama's solicitor general Neal Katyal (2019) argued. Former Attorney General Bill Barr asked Trump to stop tweeting about Department of Justice (DOJ) cases because it made his job difficult; contrarily, Trump reacted by posting multiple tweets about DOJ cases, which was regarded as "mockery" by Vox's analyst, Aaron Rupar (2020). Another example occurred during the Capitol Hill insurrection when Trump, instead of condemning the blatant acts of violence enacted by his fanatic followers, said "We love you. You're very special. Go home" (Petri, 2021, para. 3). Thus, communicative disruptions of democracy and its norms of interaction should not only be critically interrogated but also identified, analyzed, and defined.

1.7 Aims and structure

This book's objectives are manifold and focus on seeking and typifying the links between democratic disruptions and populist styles and strategies of communication; on critically reviewing and drawing lessons from the cases of Venezuela's Hugo Chávez and the US's Donald Trump; on obtaining a better understanding of the challenges posed by disruptive populist speech; and, ultimately, on building a reflection on the moral language of populist communication and discursive disruption.

I will present my critical reflections in six chapters: Chapter 1, "The disruption is discursive" introduces this study's puzzle on the novel concept of discursive disruption. Chapter 2, "Democracy, trust, truths, and lies…and style", displays the review of the literature that underpinned this study. Chapter 3, "Populist communication, discursive violence, and disrupted democracy", discusses the theoretical themes that underpin the discursive disruption framework proposed by this book. Chapter 4, "The discursive disruption framework", builds the analytical dimension of the study. In Chapter 5, "Chávez and Trump as paradigms of discursive disruption", I test the framework and execute the analysis of the two elected cases; and finally, Chapter 6, "The moral language of populist communication", showcases the implications of the study and reflects on the ethical dimension of populist communication and discursive disruption.

References

Anthony, B. (2021, October 7). *Storytelling in a digital era*. [Video]. YouTube. https://www.youtube.com/watch?v=V7uduoujEDE

Archibugi, D. (2005). The language of democracy: Vernacular or Esperanto? A comparison between the multiculturalist and cosmopolitan perspectives. *Political Studies, 53*(3), 537–555.

Ball, T., Farr, J., & Hanson, R. (1989). *Political innovation and conceptual change.* Cambridge University Press.

Bakhtin, M. M. (1981). *The dialogic imagination: Four essays* (M. Holquist, Trans.). University of Texas Press. (Original work published 1975).

BBC News. (2021, September 29). *Greta Thunberg mocks world leaders in 'blah, blah, blah' speech.* [Video]. YouTube. https://www.youtube.com/watch?v=ZwD1kG4PI0w

Biskupic, J. (2020, February 22). Trump's unbroken pattern of distain for the rule of law. *CNN.* https://edition.cnn.com/2020/02/22/politics/trump-justice-barr-rule-of-law/index.html

Block, E. (2015). *Political communication and leadership. Mimetization, Hugo Chávez and the construction of power and identity.* Routledge.

Block, E., & Negrine, R. (2017). The populist communication style: Toward a critical framework. *International Journal of Communication, 11*, 20.

Bolivar, A. (2018). *Political discourse as dialogue. A Latin American perspective.* Routledge.

Brants, K., & Voltmer, K. (Eds.). (2011). *Political communication in postmodern democracy: Challenging the primacy of politics.* Palgrave MacMillan.

Chávez, H. (1992, February 4). *Hugo Chávez 4 de Febrero 1992.* https://www.youtube.com/watch?v=VBUo-pYeVfQ

Davis, A. (2019). *Political communication. A news introduction for crisis times.* Polity.

de la Torre, C. (2017). Trump's populism: Lessons from Latin America. *Postcolonial Studies, 20*(2), 187–198.

de Waal, S. (2018). *Civil leadership as the future of leadership: Harnessing the disruptive power of citizens.* Warden Press.

Dryzek, J. (2002). *Deliberative democracy and beyond: Liberals, critics, contestations.* Oxford University Press. https://www.oxfordscholarship.com/view/10.1093/019925043X.001.0001/acprof-9780199250431

Eisen, N., Kenealy, A., Corke, S., Taussig, T., & Polyakova, A. (2019). *The democracy playbook: Preventing and reversing democratic backsliding.* Brookings. https://www.brookings.edu/research/the-democracy-playbook-preventing-and-reversing-democratic-backsliding/

Ernst, N., Blassnig, S., Engesser, S., Büchel, F., & Esser, F. (2019). Populists prefer social media over talk shows: An analysis of populist messages and stylistic elements across six countries. *Social Media + Society*. https://doi.org/10.1177/2056305118823358

Farrelly, M. (2015). *Discourse and democracy: Critical analysis of the language of government*. Routledge. https://www.amazon.com/Discourse-Democracy-Critical-Government-Routledge-ebook/dp/B00O1PQRLQ

Fitzduff, M. (2017). Introduction: All too human: The allure of Donald Trump. In M. Fitzduff (Ed.), *Why irrational politics appeals: Understanding the allure of Trump* (pp. 1–23). ABC-CLIO.

Fletcher, R., Cornia, A., & Nielsen, R. K. (2020). How polarized are online and offline news audiences? A comparative analysis of twelve countries. *The International Journal of Press/Politics*, *25*(2), 169–195. https://doi.org/10.1177/1940161219892768

Freedom House. (2019). *Democracy in retreat. Freedom in the world 2019*. https://freedomhouse.org/sites/default/files/Feb2019_FH_FITW_2019_Report_ForWeb-compressed.pdf

Freire, P. (1970). *Pedagogy of the oppressed*. Herder & Herder.

French, J. R. P. (1941). The disruption and cohesion of groups. *Journal of Abnormal and Social Psychology*, *36*(3), 361–377. https://doi.org/10.1037/h0057883

Fromm, E. (2013). *The forgotten language: An introduction to the understanding of dreams, fairy tales, and myths*. Open Road Media.

Fukuyama, F. (2000). *The great disruption. Human nature and reconstitution of the social order*. Simon and Schuster.

Fukuyama, F. (2020, January 24). Why red and blue America can't hear each other anymore. *Washington Post*. https://www.washingtonpost.com/outlook/2020/01/24/why-red-blue-america-cant-hear-each-other-anymore/?arc404=true

Gill, T. (2016). Tim Gill: Trump-Chávez comparisons "Obscure much more than they illuminate". *WOLA, Venezuelan Politics and Human Rights*. https://venezuelablog.org/tim-gill-trump-chavez-comparisons-obscure-much/

Goffman, E. (1959). *The representation of the self in everyday life*. Anchor Books.

Hameleers, M. (2019a). Partisan media, polarized audiences? A qualitative analysis of online political news and responses in the United States, UK, and The Netherlands. *International Journal of Public Opinion Research*, *31*(3), 485–505.

Hameleers, M. (2019b). The populism of online communities: Constructing the boundary between "Blameless" people and "culpable" others. *Communication Culture & Critique*, *12*(1), 147–165.

Hanson, R. L. (1989). Democracy. In T. Ball, J. Farr, & R. L. Hanson (Eds.), *Political innovation and conceptual change* (pp. 68–89). Cambridge University Press.

Harris, C. B. (2018). An American Hugo Chávez? Investigating the comparisons between Donald Trump and Latin American populists. (Undergraduate honours thesis). https://scholars.unh.edu/cgi/viewcontent.cgi?article=1437&context=honors

Hausmann, R. (2017, July 31). Venezuela's unprecedented collapse. *Project Syndicate.* https://www.project-syndicate.org/commentary/venezuela-unprecedented-economic-collapse-by-ricardo-hausmann-2017-07?barrier=accesspaylog

Hawkins, K. (2010). *Venezuela's chavismo and populism in comparative perspective.* Cambridge University Press.

Hepp, A. (2013). *Cultures of mediatization.* Polity.

Hiebert, T. (2007). The tower of Babel and the origin of the world's cultures. *Journal of Biblical Literature, 126*(1), 29–58.

Ignatius Press. (2009). *Catholic bible: Revised standard version* (1st ed.).

Information Commissioner's Office (2018). *Democracy disputed?* https://ico.org.uk/media/action-weve-taken/2259369/democracy-disrupted-110718.pdf

Katyal, N. (2019, January 30). Ex-Solicitor General: Alan Dershowitz is wrong. Trump is not above the law & should be impeached. *Democracy Now.* https://www.democracynow.org/2020/1/30/neal_katyal_impeachment_alan_dershowitz

Klein, E. (2020). *Why we're polarized?* Avid Reader Press; Simon & Schuster.

Krastev, I. (2014). *Democracy disrupted. The global politics of protest.* University of Pennsylvania Press.

Lewis, P., Barr, C., Clarke, S., Voce, A., Levett, C., & Gutiérrez, P. (2019, March 7). Revealed: The rise and rise of populist rhetoric. *The Guardian.* https://www.theguardian.com/world/ng-interactive/2019/mar/06/revealed-the-rise-and-rise-of-populist-rhetoric

Mazzoleni, G., & Bracciale, R. (2018). Socially mediated populism: The communicative strategies of political leaders on Facebook. *Palgrave Communications, 4*(1), 50.

Meireles, C. (2001). *Babel 2001.* [Large-scale sculptural installation] Tate, London. https://www.tate.org.uk/art/artworks/meireles-babel-t14041

Mounk, Y. (2018). *The people vs. democracy: Why our freedom is in danger and how to save it.* Harvard University Press.

Naím, M., & Toro, F. (2018). Venezuela's suicide. *Foreign Affairs, 97,* 126.

Norris, P. (2008). *Driving democracy: Do power-sharing institutions work?.* Cambridge University Press. https://doi.org/10.1017/CBO9780511790614

Pateman, C. (1970). *Participation and democratic theory.* Cambridge University Press.

Petri, A. (2021, January 8). We love you. You're very special. Go home. *The Washington Post.* https://www.washingtonpost.com/opinions/2021/01/07/trump-we-love-you-capitol-mob/

Rooduijn, M., & Akkerman, T. (2017). Flank attacks: Populism and left-right radicalism in Western europe. *Party Politics, 23*(3), 193–204.

Rupar, A. (2020, February 21). Trump is making a mockery of Bill Barr. *Vox.* https://www.vox.com/2020/2/21/21146051/trump-bill-barr-tweets-doj-cases

Schmidt, E., & Cohen, J. (2010). The digital disruption connectivity and the diffusion of power. *Foreign Affairs.* http://cddrl.fsi.stanford.edu/sites/default/files/schmidt_the_digital_disruption.pdf

Stiegler, B. (2019). *The age of disruption: Technology and madness in computational capitalism.* Polity.

Tharoor, I. (2020, February 14). Trump's authoritarian style is remaking America. *The Washington Post.* https://www.washingtonpost.com/world/2020/02/14/trumps-authoritarian-style-is-remaking-america/

Thompson, M. (2016). From Trump to Brexit rhetoric: How today's politicians have got away with words? *The Guardian.* https://www.theguardian.com/books/2016/aug/27/from-trump-to-brexit-rhetoric-how-todays-politicians-have-got-away-with-words

Thompson, M. (2017). *Enough said: What's gone wrong with the language of politics?* St. Martin's Press.

United Nations Human Rights, Office of the High Commissioner (2019, July 4). *UN Human Rights report on Venezuela urges immediate measures to halt and remedy grave rights violations.* https://www.ohchr.org/EN/NewsEvents/Pages/DisplayNews.aspx?NewsID=24788&LangID=E

Walter, R. (2008). Foucault and radical deliberative democracy. *Australian Journal of Political Science, 43*(3), 531–546.

Vollmer, H. (2013). *The sociology of disruption, disaster and social change: Punctuated cooperation.* Cambridge University Press.

Young, I. M. (1997a). *Intersecting voices.* Princeton University Press.

Young, I. M. (1997b). Difference as a resource for democratic communication. In J. Bohman & W. Rehg (Eds.), *Deliberative democracy: Essays on reason and politics* (pp. 383–404). MIT Press. https://ebookcentral-proquest-com.ezproxy.library.uq.edu.au/lib/uql/detail.action?docID=3338820#

2 Democracy, trust, truths, lies...and style

Concerns for erosions of democracy are not new in the political communication field or in the news media's agenda. Brants and Voltmer (2011) asked a question in 2011 that was as valid then as it is today: "What does it mean for modern democracy when those in power lose their ability to communicate with those they are supposed to represent" (p. 1). They suggested that the mediatization of politics would lead to an increase of political cynicism, disenchantment, and the use of citizen-empowering, bottom-up internet spaces. Although their predictions have proved to be partly true, power relations in digital and multi-fragmented social media spaces are not as bottom up as Brants and Voltmer (2011) anticipated. Social media platforms have been shown to be fertile grounds for media-savvy populist leaders, skillful peddlers of identity, resentment, and discontent, ranting adversarial and in some cases conspiratorial messages, delivered to audiences eager to listen to those who tap into their political frustrations.

A few years later, Bennett and Pfetsch (2018), advanced the concept of "disrupted public spheres", a term that they used to describe the "disconnection of publics from institutions of press and politics due to the hollowing of center parties and social divides" (p. 243). These scholars called for deeper political communication research on these topics. Their focus on the decline of center-ground voices is important, as extreme positions have now become the order of the day when citizens are often prompted to take sides, especially in social media interactions. In the similar vein, Waisbord (2018) highlighted the role played by populist leaders in eroding democracy. He viewed populists' "patterns of exclusion" (p. 34) and "agonistic view of politics" (p. 23), as "opposed" to the idea of a communication commons, shared dialogic spaces where ideas could be discussed openly and reasonably. Waisbord (2018) suggested that critical communication scholars should pay more attention to the analysis of the adversarial

DOI: 10.4324/9781003118602-2

populist communication ethos. This book is a response to these and other scholars who have expressed concerns about the state of democracy and its links with communicative processes and populism. This second chapter reviews the set of themes that inspired and together constitute the background of the study.

2.1　Trust, truths, and lies in politics

Functionalist and pluralist scholars define trust as *human interaction* that is not only necessary in everyday human relationships but also has become fundamental in our intensive and increasingly frequent mediatized exchanges. In this light, trust is represented as an optimistic, rather idealistic concept, key to the construction of cooperation, community, communication, and engagement. Robert Putnam, Robert Leonardi, and Raffaella Nanetti (1993), for example, interconnected trust with social capital and civic engagement building. Their normative idea of trust embodies the belief that our counterparts will not act in a harmful but in a beneficial, reliable way.

In the same line, but from a more pragmatic, business orientated perspective, Edelman (2021c), a multinational, research communication company that has conducted surveys on democracy and trust for over 20 years, defined trust as "the ultimate currency in the relationships that all institutions...build with their stakeholders" (para. 1). Edelman (2021c) suggested that trust constitutes an "insurance against competitive disruption" (para. 2) adding that "without trust, credibility is lost, and reputation can be threatened" (para. 2). However, Edelman's idealistic argument raises a question: Is trust really an "insurance" against communicative or discursive disruption? Or rather a blind or irrational trust in some leaders can become an accelerator?

A different, more critical and skeptical, political sociology approach to trust was provided by William Gamson (1968), who explained it as "the creator of collective power" (p. 42), arguing that "the loss of trust is the loss of system power, the loss of a generalized capacity for authorities to commit resources to attain collective goals." (p. 42). Gamson's (1968) definition equalizes trust with power, an essential factor in the way people engage with government and politics. Trust is a must-have factor in democracy that ensures the legitimation of political actors and institutions as well as their discourses, policy, and actions. Trust helps political actors of different kinds build power and identity.

Therefore, the idea of trust is embedded in issues of power, consent, and legitimacy. Gramsci's (1971) idea of legitimacy, for instance is based on building moral and intellectual leadership to reinforce bonds among the likeminded and to exert domination or force against opponents when necessary (p. 57). In this context, as a way of example, the legitimacy of Latin American populist caudillos, was mainly personal and symbolic, more based on their rhetorical skills, patriotic identity, and charisma than on the rule of law or formal institutions (see Lynch, 1992).

The foregoing discussion explains why, drawing on Charles Taylor's (2002) concept of the imaginary, I suggest trust as an imaginary, or rather imaginaries, embodying "that common understanding that makes possible common practices and a widely shared sense of legitimacy" (p. 106). In today's disrupted democratic societies, where Babelian media infrastructures and antidialogic political relations reign, it would be idealistic or naïve to assume that citizens with different beliefs, backgrounds, and socio-political worldviews will share the same discourses or reach consensus all the time, or indeed at any time. Different, even conflicting imaginaries of constitution, democracy and trust coexist in the same society, and this is not as negative to society as some might think. As Young (1997) argued, it is pluralism and difference, instead of monologic, single-sided, identity politics, that guarantees healthier democracies. What matters is that those with different views maintain a tolerant dialogue with each other. It can be argued that pluralism, and especially communication within plurality, is at the core of a desired (but probably idealistic) shared moral and political language, discussed in Chapter 1.

Among other reasons (better explained and justified in Chapter 4), I selected this book's two case studies—Venezuela's Hugo Chávez and the US's Donald Trump—for the conflicting imaginaries of democracy and trust that can be identified within their respective political cultures. Clashes represented, for example, by the bizarre coexistence of two completely opposed political worldviews and even presidents in a Venezuela engaged in never-ending discursive struggles between populist chavismo and antichavismo for over two decades (see Anderson, 2019; Hellinger, 2019, among others).

In the US, the conflicting interpretations of Trump's so called "Big Lie" about the 2020 electoral results (by assuring that he won "in a landslide" but was prevented to take power by a "massive" electoral fraud that "stole" the elections from him), illustrate one of the Trumpian imaginaries of trust and democracy at play. Political and media commentators have represented Trump's claim as the "Big Lie", alluding to similarities with Hilter's *Mein Kampf* cliché definition that enabled the Nazi dictator to support and legitimize his regime's persecution and extermination of Jews. The Big Lie was reaffirmed in Trump's (2021) "Save America" speech, used by his second impeachment panel as one of the igniting events giving rise to the January 6, 2021 Capitol Hill insurrection (Naylor, 2021). Multiple footage and photos and subsequent analyses and interpretations of the Capitol Hill siege by a strongly critical legacy media, notably *CNN* ("Former QAnon supporter to Cooper", 2021), *The New York Times* (Barry et al., 2021), and the *Washington Post* (Harwell et al., 2021), tried to make sense of how and why a cult-like Trumpian mob stormed Congress. Many interpretations were given, but dominant legacy media accounts suggested that this mob, mainly formed by QAnon, Proud Boys, Oath Keepers, and other ultra conservative and white supremacist organizations, stormed the Capitol, fueled by Trump's "massive" electoral fraud and "stolen election" discourses; also, by conspiracy theories accusing the left or "liberal" political and media elites of belonging to pedophilic or communist cabals. The interview conducted by *CNN* journalist Anderson Cooper ("Former QAnon supporter to Cooper", 2021) with a former QAnon member illustrates this imaginary underpinned by a messianic representation of former president Trump. In stark contrast, the second imaginary of American democracy is illustrated by the deeply outraged, albeit conventional and sedate, center-ground view of the same event by President Joe Biden (2021), who said,

> Let me be very clear: the scenes of chaos at the Capitol do not represent who we are. What we are seeing is a small number of extremists dedicated to lawlessness. This is not dissent, it's disorder. It borders on sedition, and it must end. Now.

However, as Mogelson (2021a; 2021b) suggested in his video reportage and analysis of the January 6 insurrection, conventional politicians, such as President Biden, are reluctant to openly recognize the existence of the "other", neglecting to admit that the insurrectionists, as unlawful as they were, are also part of the American "who we are". Trump's Big Lie not only refers to issues of trust, but also raises questions about the use of truth and lies in politics.

Like Trump, Hugo Chávez was also accused of lying throughout his rule. The original and probably the most blatant of Chávez's lies was his initial denial about being a socialist. In a TV interview with Peruvian TV presenter Jaime Baily, published in 1998, the year of his first electoral campaign, candidate Chávez indicated, "No, I am not a socialist… I believe that today's world requires a jump beyond socialism and even beyond savage capitalism, as Pope John Paul II calls it. It is a humanist project" (Chávez, 1998). Thus, Chávez tried to initially hide his "Socialism of the 21st century" project despite his close relationship with Cuba's Fidel Castro. Chávez visited Castro in Havana for the first time less than 15 days after he took office in January 1999. However, political culture studies such as, for example, the investigation sponsored by think tank Pensamiento y Acción (1996) indicated that Venezuelans had traditionally rejected socialism in favor of democracy as the best system of governance. Thus, the rationale behind candidate Chávez's original lie is rather simple—as Univision journalist Jorge Ramos (2007) suggested later, Chávez "lied to get to power" (para. 11) through defusing potential voters that he knew would reject his socialist tendencies. Chávez created and promoted what he called "Bolivarian socialism of the 21st century", whereby he manipulated the myth surrounding Venezuela's independence hero Simon Bolivar, a significant part of the country's political culture, to his own power ends. Chávez used Bolivar as a discursive tool in what later became, paraphrasing Gramsci (1971), a *permanent revolution*; or rather, a permanent struggle led by a messianic leader to weaken and eliminate democratic opposition to maintain his, and his clique's power. Chávez used the power of his words and charisma to build the trust and legitimacy necessary to disrupt and overturn Venezuelan democracy, within democracy.

The use of lies in politics was studied by Hannah Arendt (1972) in her analysis of the Pentagon Papers case and the role of Robert McNamara and the civil service in the Vietnam war. Arendt (1972) argued that the discourses constructed by key American political players about Vietnam were governed by a "game of deceptions and falsehoods" driven by "mistaken patriotism" (p. 10). Arendt's argument about mistaken patriotism could also be applied to the analysis of the ultranationalist discourses vociferated by both, the "Make America First" (MAGA) Trump following and Bolivarian chavista voters. Myths and lies are part of the imaginaries and discourses forming the political culture of a nation and are often more trusted than factual truths. As Arendt (1972) also suggested,

Factual truths are never compellingly true. The historian knows how vulnerable is the whole texture of facts in which we spend our daily life; it is always in danger of being perforated by single lies or torn to shreds by the organized lying of groups, nations, or classes, or denied or distorted, often carefully covered up by realms of falsehoods or simply allowed to fall into oblivion.

(p. 5)

Blurry representations of trust, lies and truth in politics explain why, despite having been initially elected under the rules of democracy of their respective countries, both Donald Trump and Hugo Chávez, from the beginning of their respective rules sought to erode their constituents' trust in democracy by building parallel discourses and imaginaries where lies and truth merge in a sea of misinformation delivered through politicized media and social media spaces (see Block, 2015; Human Rights Watch, 2008a; 2008b; 2012; among others).

2.2 The eroded discourses of democracy

After situating the issues of trust, truth, and lies in politics, I expand next on some of the most relevant results rendered by public opinion investigations about erosions and dysfunctions of contemporary democracy. These investigations were carried out or sponsored by relevant research centers, think tanks, and news media outlets, such as the Pew Research Centre (Connaughton et al., 2020; Wike et al., 2019); Freedom House (2018; 2019; Repucci & Slipowitz, 2020; Schenkkan, 2020); IDEA (2019); Edelman Trust Barometer (2019; 2020); Social Science Research Council (SSRC; Blair, 2018); Reuters' Digital News Report (Newman, 2020); The Economist Intelligence Unit (EIU; "Global Democracy has", 2020); *The Guardian* (Lewis et al., 2019); and the UK Information Commissioner's Office (ICO, 2018), the last two were commented on in Chapter 1.

Before starting the review of the surveys, I want to acknowledge criticism in the literature—mainly among academics, media commentators and competing pollsters—about the accuracy, bias, or partisanship of some of the indicators and results. For example, Freedom House (n.d.), a think tank founded by Eleanor Roosevelt in 1941 under the sponsorship of the United Nations (UN), has been criticized for the use of Americanized indicators and their definition of democracy, as well as rankings driven by whether surveyed countries were or were not close allies of the US. Freedom House has also been accused of partisanship toward the "progressive left" by Conservative think tank The Heritage Foundation (2018). The EIU's Democracy Index ("Global Democracy has", 2020) has also been represented as "riddled" with biases due to the obscurity of the anonymous "experts" they use as respondents in their yearly ranking exercises (Tasker, 2016). Notwithstanding, I will use some of their results for two reasons: First, most of these centers have rated democracy worldwide for decades as they have the resources and knowhow to conduct quantitative research in over 100 countries; and second, because, taken together their results and narratives point to congruent global and country-specific trends vis-à-vis democracy.

With slight variants, the main indicators used to measure democracy by most of the organizations reviewed in this chapter are consistent with the five indicators created in 2006 by the EIU, namely: "electoral process and pluralism; civil liberties; the functioning of government; political participation; and political culture" (Kekic, 2007, para. 11). Depending on the results, the EIU ranks countries as "full democracies", "flawed democracies", "hybrid regimes", and "authoritarian regimes" (see "Global Democracy has", 2020), which although may involve some culturally problematic classifications, I will use them as approximations to the political situation in some countries, especially in the US and Venezuela, my two case studies. I summarize a review of the rankings next.

2.2.1 Review of key studies

Freedom House (2018), was perhaps the first to report that in 2017 democracy faced its most severe crisis in decades. The basic tenets of democracy (including guarantees of free and fair elections, the rights of minorities, freedom of the press, and the rule of law) came under attack around the world. Seventy-one countries suffered net declines in political rights and civil liberties. In addition, the US retreated from its traditional role as both a champion and an exemplar of democracy amid an accelerating decline in American political rights and civil liberties.

The following year, Freedom House released their Freedom of the World report, entitled *Democracy in Retreat* (2019), mentioned in Chapter 1, which confirmed a decline in global democratic freedom for the 13th consecutive year. The report also confirmed that long-standing democracies "have been shaken by populist forces that reject basic principles like separation of powers and target minorities for discriminatory treatment" (Freedom House, 2019, para. 2), suggesting that populists' "unilateral reflexes" and ongoing attacks of the news media contributed to democracy's decline and polarization.

The Pew Research Centre (Wike et al., 2019) equally pointed to widespread dissatisfaction with democracy worldwide. The study, which polled 27 countries, revealed that "anger at political elites, economic dissatisfaction and anxiety about rapid social changes have fueled political upheaval in regions around the world in recent years" (para. 1). They registered anger against the establishment from people that identify with "both the right and left of the political spectrum" (Wike et al.,

2019). These are audiences that have tended to challenge norms, values, and conventions as they are "unhappy with the way their democracies are working" (para. 28). One year later, in 2020, the Pew Research Centre (Connaughton et al., 2020) indicated that the dissatisfaction with democracy had increased and strengthened in the 34 countries in which they conducted their investigations with 52% of surveyed people expressing dissatisfaction with democracy, compared with 44% who were satisfied, blaming elected officials for neglecting what voters think or feel; only 32% agreed that elected officials cared for them. Disenchantment with democracy increased even in some of the most established democracies, such as the UK (69%) and the US (59%).

IDEA's *Global State of Democracy* (2019) report indicated that "the share of countries experiencing democratic erosion has more than doubled in the past decade compared to the decade before" (p. 2). Relevant to my book, IDEA's (2019) report suggested that Venezuela represented "the most severe democratic backsliding case in the past four decades. Venezuela is the only country that has gone from being a democracy with high levels of Representative Government in 1975 to a non-democracy" (p. 2).

In 2020, the EIU ("Global Democracy has", 2020) report, which rated 167 countries, reaffirmed that democracy had been severely "eroded around the world in the past year" (para. 1) with a global score of 5.44/10, which was "the lowest recorded since the index began in 2006" (para. 1). The report suggested that only 22 countries could be represented as "full democracies", highlighting that "more than a third of the world population…still live under authoritarian rule" (para. 1).

The EIU study also indicated that the US had fallen from "full democracy" to position number 25, a "flawed democracy", with an index of 7.92/10, a significant decrease in comparison with the 8.22/10 obtained in 2006. A flawed democracy is one where there are free and fair elections but where opposition or media are often antagonized by government, and there are some problems of participation and functioning of governance. Consistent with IDEA's (2019) results, the EIU's ("Global Democracy has", 2020) report placed chavista Venezuela (under president Nicolas Maduro) at the bottom, in position 140 of the democracy chart, characterizing this country as an "authoritarian regime", that is, nations where pluralism is limited or does not exist. In 2006, when Hugo Chávez was in power, the country had been slightly better positioned as a "hybrid regime"—countries where the opposition is regularly intimidated, the rule of law and the media are under pressure, and there are frequent electoral frauds—with an index of 5.42/10.

The *2021 Edelman Trust Barometer* report released in January 2021 indicated that as the pandemic year 2020 advanced, some contradictory political decisions regarding physical and socioeconomic restrictions taken in various countries increased misinformation and hence the lack of trust in democracy; mistrust spread and impacted not only political institutions and leaders, media and social media, but also businesses and their CEOs. Edelman's (2021a) report suggested that there is a crisis of leadership and that the spread of misinformation led them to declare 2021 as the year of "information bankruptcy", as people "do not know where to turn for reliable information" (para. 1).

Edelman's 2021 results flagged a trend that has been developing for some years. In 2020, *Reuters' Digital News Report* (Newman, 2020) had stressed that "global concerns about misinformation remain high" (para.10) and that some audiences were increasingly troubled about truthfulness in digital environments. A year earlier, in 2019, the Pew Research Centre also released a report that although it focused only on the US, suggested relevant trends: 68% of surveyed Americans believed that "made-up news" was greatly affecting their trust in political institutions and, even worse, 54% believed that it was also affecting their trust in each other, "causing significant harms to the nation" (Dimock, 2019, para. 4).

Therefore, distrust in politics and media greatly increased between 2017 and 2020, which, from a critical communication perspective, raises two sets of concerns: On the one side, growing misinformation and circulation of contradictory and extreme views, illustrated by the latest 2021 Edelman Trust Barometer Press Release (2021b), suggested that audiences were confused about *what* information and *which* voices to trust for dependable information. A majority of respondents believed that government leaders (57%), business leaders (56%), and journalists (59%) were "purposively trying to mislead people by saying things they know are false" (para. 1). The world was thirsty for information about the deadly COVID-19 pandemic, but instead of relying on media, media trust plummeted, especially with respect to social media (35%) and owned media (41%). Trust in traditional or legacy media also decreased eight points (53%) but proved to be more trusted than nonjournalistic social media information. Decreasing distrust in media and social media in 2020 and 2021 was also highlighted by several researchers working for the Pew Research Centre; the *Reuters' Digital News Report* (Newman, 2020), and the EIU Democracy Index ("Global Democracy has", 2020).

On the other side, misinformation and mistrust have led to deeper divisions, disenchantment, and polarization among citizens or audiences.

Growing political divisions are clearly reflected in the news sources that citizens use for political information. For example, the Pew Research Center revealed a deep party polarization in American audiences' media habits or engagement, with Republicans relying on *Fox News* and Democrats on *CNN* as their main news sources; this led to "one-sided audiences" that use likeminded media outlets fitting in with their party and ideology identification (Jurkowitz et al., 2020). After the 2020 elections, some Republicans started to blame the media and social media for political divisions, misinformation, and democratic distrust. For example, Republican pollster, Frank Luntz, in an interview with *Fox News'* Howard Kurtz (see Hains, 2021; Tight Shot, 2021) expressed disgust and despair over the state of media, especially cable news, which have been just "preaching to the choir" (Hains, 2021, para. 1).

Looking at these results critically and in perspective, it is important to add that the decline of trust in democracy and media started years before the pandemic and years before Chávez or Trump came to power. They, and other populist leaders who have won elections, are rather *the outcome* of antipolitical currents, public distrust in democracy and politics. Rather than viewing populism as an *effect*, as it is often studied, populism is an indicator of other problems, grievances, and deficiencies existing in the polity that are rooted in democracy itself; problems and grievances that are used by populist players in their speeches to decry the political and media elites, the establishment and democracy as a system. Populists tap into people's antipolitical emotions.

Moreover, blaming the news media for the decline of democracy is not a new phenomenon either. For years, politicians have blamed journalists and journalists have blamed politicians when things do not work or are not publicized in the way these actors want. This mutual blaming game, which historically started with modern democracy and journalism, was defined by Brants et al. (2010) as the "spiral of mistrust" (p. 6), a political communication interplay that became normalized by popular culture. The verbal squabbles and mistrust went on, often illustrated by everyday cynical and somehow predictable late show narratives and satire. The Jon Stewart Show was a popular culture paradigm of this era and became a heated source of academic discussion (see, for example Hariman, 2007 or Warner, 2007). But this type of politician-journalist interplay very seldom escalated to the point to consider each other an "enemy".

While the cynical banter of the past was accepted, often enjoyed, and even regarded as necessary for democracy and accountability by the political and media elites (who then controlled the political conversation agenda), newer and more brutal versions of the clash emerged, currently and notably represented, for example, by hate speech and cancel culture narratives. In the case of the US, the decline of trust in democracy greatly extends to social media platforms; the Pew Research Center revealed that 64% of Americans believe that social media have had a "negative effect" on the country's mood, particularly regarding misinformation, hatred and harassment, fomenting partisanship, polarization and fanaticism, with users "believing everything they see" (Auxier, 2020, para. 3). And another, more specific study, also by the Pew Research Center, suggested that the 61% of Republicans who "relied on Trump for news" (Jurkowitz, 2021, para. 2) were more likely to be concerned by fraud and rigged elections.

Something similar happened in Venezuela, an embattled country which, despite corruption and mismanagement accusations and events, used to have a reasonably well-regarded and functioning representative democracy from the 1960s to the 1990s, when Chávez attempted his failed military coup (1992). At the end of the decade, in 1998, the 'Comandante' won the presidency by participating in democratic elections. Since then, a permanently divided opposition has unsuccessfully tried to debunk Chávez's disruptive discourse and defeat his disastrous populist legacy. An increasingly authoritarian government, censorship and absence of dialogue between government, opposition, and news media groups have prevented Venezuela from advancing toward a political change. A deeply divided country under censorship, severe news media restrictions and penalizations, has made social media platforms a basic need. However, the complete reliance on media platforms for information has made Venezuelan audiences more susceptible and liable to be misled or fooled by media-savvy and power-thirsty leaders and factions on all sides of the political and media spectra. "A distorted media reality" (Latouche, 2017, para. 9) has shaken up a Venezuela which, like many world countries, has a "fake news problem too" (para. 13); fake news and distorted reality experienced on Facebook, Instagram, Twitter, and private messaging sites, such as WhatsApp, Messenger, and Telegram. In his study of the Venezuelan media environment, Latouche (2017) argued,

> Reality in this crisis-beset nation is mediated by unconfirmed, often tendentious, information, causing anxiety and overwhelming our ability to process. The alterative facts distort perceptions and stoke expectations (or disappointments), depending entirely on the sources one accesses and the personal capacity to distinguish fiction from truth.
>
> (para. 13–14).

Thus, generalized mistrust in politics and democracy—also known as antipolitics—has existed in Venezuela for decades, even before Chávez's presidency, and are part of the imaginaries that comprise the political culture of the nation. As I argued elsewhere, Chávez did not bring antipolitics with him; antipolitical discourses are part of the reason Chávez won the elections in 1998 (Block, 2015). And the antipolitical sentiment remains today: Pollsters, such as Delphos' director, Felix Seijas, have indicated that although the opposition retains 57.9% of the voting intention, there is great mistrust in the prevailing electoral system controlled by members of Chavismo (Lopez, 2019). Paradoxically, in Delphos' 2019 poll, Venezuelans cried out for new leaders capable of gaining their trust and of providing a new route to alleviate their vital problems (Lopez, 2019). Moreover, Consultores 21's director, Saul Cabrera, argued that while the population wants a change of government in a two to one proportion, which would guarantee a change of government in any democratic country, the authoritarian populist chavista regime have prevented the country from having transparent elections (cited in Martinez, 2018). Divisions within the opposition have not helped the situation either and although seven out of ten Venezuelans say that it is better to vote than to abstain, four out of ten do not trust the highest electoral body—Consejo Nacional Electoral (CNE)—which is viewed as having perpetrated electoral fraud for years and is incapable of guaranteeing free elections. Thus, generalized distrust in the regime, CNE, and even in and among the same opposition leaders has politically immobilized Venezuelans, who, despite numerous electoral processes, some of which have been controversial and unsuccessfully contested by opposition leaders and academics, have been in a disruptive and rather tragic cul-de-sac throughout the chavista era.

Mistrust in politics and media, misinformation, polarization, and disenchantment talk set the ground for populists to emerge and succeed. Populists feed off antipolitical divisions and unhappiness, especially in countries with weak political institutions.

2.3 Populism versus democracy

Earlier academic research analyzed populism vis-à-vis democracy, mainly as a sort of sickness or aberration. Margaret Canovan (2002) classically represented populism as the shadow of democracy, whereas Arditi (2004) preferred to call populism the "specter" of democracy. Norris and Inglehart (2019) proposed populism as a "cultural backlash" from traditionalists against the threats represented by the rise of civil rights, political correctness, and liberal values. Van Aelst et al. (2017), in their study on populist communication, reflected on the fundamental changes occurring in media environments and political communication systems. Among the democratic implications of such changes, these researchers indicated "(1) declining supply of political information, (2) declining quality of news, (3) increasing media concentration, (4) increasing fragmentation and polarization, (5) increasing relativism, and (6) increasing inequality in political knowledge" (Van Aelst et al., 2017, p. 3). Both views of populism, by Norris and Inglehart (2019) and Van Aelst et al. (2017), included relevant clues as to how populist communication and communicators have played key roles in the decline of democratic discourses.

Although discourse scholar Ruth Wodak's (2015) concept of populism mainly refers to right-wing populist parties, it is nonetheless consistent with some of the definitions that view populism as a "form of rhetoric" (p. 1) or communication, consisting of specific content focused on the construction of fear and "scapegoats" "that are blamed for threatening or actually damaging our societies" (p. 1). Wodak (2015) also highlighted how populist parties thrive on a "politics of fear" (p. 2) and endorsed what she called "the arrogance of ignorance" (p. 2) as their discourse appeals to "common-sense and anti-intellectualism" (p. 2) pushing toward a return to pre-modernist thinking. Wodak's (2015) description of the right-wing populist rhetoric, I argue, can also be used for left-wing forms of populism that are equally based on the construction of elite enemies, and thrive on fear, ignorance and anti-intellectualism. A description that, I suggest, can be applied to both Trump and Chávez.

From a sociological/postcolonial perspective, de la Torre (2017) reflected on Trump's populism vis-à-vis two cases of Latin American populism (Hugo Chávez and Ecuador's Rafael Correa). De la Torre (2017) explained that whereas both Chávez and Correa "undermined democracy from within" (p. 195) by taking over political institutions in their respective countries, Trump, in a short time and despite the US's stronger institutions, has started to build a "disfigured democracy", by "damaging the democratic public sphere" (p. 195).

Thus, populists have managed to disrupt, change, and even destroy democracy *within* democracy. Their innate rejection of the separation of powers, tolerance to opposing views and pluralism impregnate their actions and also their talk when they are in positions of power, which is another element to be considered for the discursive disruption framework.

My past investigations on the populist communication style with emeritus professor Ralph Negrine (see Block & Negrine, 2017) suggested that, at least in Venezuela, democracy's failure to satisfy the expectations of all voters, mismanagement of resources, corruption, and especially, little or no effective connection of the political elites with voters, led to Hugo Chávez's enduring success. We argued that the main appeal of populist leaders lies in the way they communicate and connect with the left behind, dissatisfied or disenfranchised. Populists tend to "bond" with their supporters *not in spite of,* but *precisely because* of their antagonistic, disruptive, and abrasive talk, different to that used by sedate traditional politicians. Populists connect with their voters, fans or followers, either because "there is something that is not working in their polity or because they feel threatened by change" (Block & Negrine, 2017, p. 183). The "emotional bond" is mainly built through language, words, through a strategic style of communication. We suggested that it is time to deal with populism, and populist communication, not as a sort of sickness or aberration but as a phenomenon that is *part of democracy* that corrodes democracy from within eventually becoming its antithesis in the process.

From a different perspective, linguistics and discourse professor Adriana Bolivar (2018), who studies political discourse in terms of dialogue and confrontation, suggested that populist verbal actions can have significant implications in material or pragmatic life, as has happened in Latin America. This argument's strength, which has some of its roots in Austin's (2020), Bakhtin's (1981), and Freire's (1970) views on the power of words and how they can trigger material actions, led me to propose discursive disruption as a process or logic that typifies how populist communication has had a disruptive impact, both symbolically and materially, on democracy in some countries. Also, it led me to propose a framework that helps identify, analyze, and understand such processes.

2.4 Critical political communication, style, and discursive violence

Classically, political communication was defined by the legendary Jay Blumler (2011) as a discipline that links "political culture, political actors, media organizations, including the roles played by journalists within them, and bodies of increasingly heterogeneous and varyingly involved citizens" (p. 9). Blumler (2011) and also Voltmer (2006) suggested that political communication helps study, critically analyze, and build frameworks to understand power relationships in different groups or societies in specific contexts and times. Political communication also helps to understand and explain why these relations *matter.*

It is precisely the study of power relations and culture that makes political communication a *critical* discipline. Pfetsch (2004) added the issue of culture to political communication; she advanced the concept of political communication culture as "an essential component of the political culture of a country" (p. 346).

Using a critical political communication approach, I interrogate the main elements and characteristics of the populist communication style, and the ways in which such style may have contributed to disrupt democracy, and especially the flow of communication within democracy, in my two case studies. In this context, I analyze the way some populist leaders, such as Chávez and Trump, use words, identity and media to skirt, interrupt, bypass, or change some of their countries' democratic conventions to suit their power goals.

Therefore, critical political communication also involves the study of certain *styles*, which explains why political actors, populist actors in this case, say what they say, the contexts or situations in which they say it, and the communicative strategies and channels or platforms of communication they use to put their messages across in power relations. As Negrine and Papathanassopoulos (2011) suggested, political communication critically studies both "the means and practices whereby the communication of politics takes place" (p. 41), and the way power relationships are performed and negotiated over the control of the agenda. This claim in turn reaffirms that there are different "styles" of approaching and practicing political communication.

Therefore, the concept of "style" is particularly relevant to understand populist communication and populist communicators, like Chávez and Trump. Historian Richard Hofstadter (2008), in a study about the "paranoid style" in American politics, defined style as "the way in which ideas are believed and advocated" by political actors—in this case, populist actors—rather than "the truth or falsity of their content" (p. 5). Although this definition concentrates on purely stylistic features (the *how*), it is relevant in today's "post truth" era, when so called "alternative facts", or lies, play an important role in the construction of some political discourses in democracy (Thompson, 2020).

Anthropologist and sociolinguist Michael Silverstein's (2003) concept seems, however, more pertinent to this book's study, as he saw style as the way political actors communicate image or identity, which explains why he believed style, identity, and message should not be studied separately; for him, style means "The substance of it all" (p. 5). Style, thus, is not pure form but embodies message and identity in the same package. Finally, Hariman's (1995) description of political style is, in a way, a summary, or deconstructions of the definitions above, as he defined style in terms of (a) a repertoire of rhetorical conventions, (b) the construction of individual and collective identities and power, and (c) practices and media of communication used by political actors to persuade and connect with audiences.

The foregoing discussion led me to build a working definition of *political communication style* as patterns of political speech and messaging that embody meaning, language, identity, and tone that together help political actors to connect with their audiences through mediated and unmediated channels of communication. Populist imaginaries of truth, trust and lies, for example, involve antagonistic, antidialogic, emotional antipolitical appeals that enable populist speakers to connect with politically disenchanted audiences. In the same way that poet Roman Jakobson (1923, as cited in Esposito et al., 2018, p. 291) represented the style of poetry as "organized violence committed on ordinary speech", I represent the populist communication style as *discursive violence committed on democratic political communication*. This discussion, in turn, calls for a reflection on the discursive character of politics.

From different perspectives, Foucault (1972), van Dijk (1997), Fairclough (2003), Wodak (2015), and Bolivar (2003, 2018) shared the view that politics is discursively and linguistically constructed. Political discourse is about *discursive* ways of "doing politics" involving "all participants in the political process" (van Dijk, 1997, p. 13). Politicians, citizens, news media and their audiences, and interest groups interact in politics and participate in relationships of power and discursive practices within the polity. Thus, as I argued in Chapter 1, *disruptions in democracy are initially discursive.*

Latin American linguist and discourse scholar, Adriana Bolivar (2018, p. 1) reflected on "discourse as dialogue", situating dialogue at the heart of social interactions between humans in the cocreation of discourse. As Bolívar (2018) suggested, verbal actions have a pragmatic impact on material or pragmatic life, whereby confrontation, as a key element "brings to the surface impoliteness and verbal aggression" (p. 105). Impoliteness and verbal aggression are two of the favorite discursive tactics used by populist players Chávez and Trump; discursive violence is a key element of their respective communicative styles. This explains why I argue that populism should not be solely understood as an ideology or aberration of democracy, but as *a political communication style, a speech strategy, which at its worst is violence perpetrated against the language of democracy, within democracy.* This topic will be further explored in Chapter 3.

References

Anderson, J. L. (2019, June 3). Venezuela's two presidents collide. *The New Yorker.* https://www.newyorker.com/magazine/2019/06/10/venezuelas-two-presidents-collide

Arditi, B. (2004). Populism as a spectre of democracy: A response to Canovan. *Political Studies, 52*(1), 135–143.

Arendt, H. (1972). Lying in politics. *Crises of the Republic.* Harvest Books (pp. 3–46).

Austin, J. L. (2020). *How to do things with words.* Barakaldo Books.

Auxier, B. (2020, October 15). 64% of Americans say social media have a mostly negative effect on the way things are going in the U.S. today. *Pew Research Centre.* https://www.pewresearch.org/topics/social-media/

Bakhtin, M. M. (1981). *The dialogic imagination: Four essays* (M. Holquist, Trans.). University of Texas Press (Original work published 1975).

Barry, D., McIntire, M., & Rosenberg, M. (2021, January 9). 'Our President wants us here': The mob that stormed the Capitol. *The New York Times.* https://www.nytimes.com/2021/01/09/us/capitol-rioters.html

Bennett, W. L., & Pfetsch, B. (2018). Rethinking political communication in a time of disrupted public spheres. *Journal of Communication, 68*(2), 243–253. https://doi.org/10.1093/joc/jqx017

Biden, J. [@JoeBiden]. (2021, January 6). *Let me be very clear: the scenes of chaos at the Capitol do not represent who we are. What we are* Twitter. https://bit.ly/3sBxYxo

Blair, R. (2018, August 7). Introducing "Democratic Erosion". *Items: Insights from the Social Sciences.* https://items.ssrc.org/introducing-democratic-erosion/

Block, E. (2015). *Political communication and leadership. Mimetization, Hugo Chávez and the construction of power and identity.* Routledge.

Block, E., & Negrine, R. (2017). The populist communication style: Toward a critical framework. *International Journal of Communication, 11*, 20.

Blumler, J. (2011). In praise of holistic empiricism. In K. Brants, & K. Voltmer (Eds.), *Political communication in postmodern democracy: Challenging the primacy of politics* (pp. 9–12). Palgrave MacMillan

Bolívar, A. (2003). Nuevos géneros discursivos en la política: El caso de alo presidente. In B. Leda (Ed.), *Análisis crítico del discurso: Perspectivas latinoamericanas* (pp. 101–130). Frasis editors.

Bolivar, A. (2018). *Political discourse as dialogue. A Latin American perspective.* Routledge.

Brants, K., & Voltmer, K. (Eds.). (2011). *Political communication in postmodern democracy: Challenging the primacy of politics.* Palgrave MacMillan.

Brants, K., de Vreese, C., Möller, J., & van Praag, P. (2010). The real spiral of cynicism? Symbiosis and mistrust between politicians and journalists. *The International Journal of Press/Politics, 15*(1), 25–40. https://doi.org/10.1177/1940161209351005

Canovan, M. (2002). Taking politics to the people: Populism as the ideology of democracy. In Y. Meny, & Y. Surel (Eds.), *Democracies and the populist challenge* (pp. 25–44). Palgrave Macmillan.

Chávez, H. (1998, April 11). *Interview with Hugo Chávez's during the presidential campaign of 1998.* [Video]. YouTube. http://youtu.be/mE8o4Yxh70

Connaughton, A., Kent, N., & Schumacher, S. (2020, February 27). How people around the world see democracy in 8 charts. *Pew Research Center.* https://www.pewresearch.org/fact-tank/2020/02/27/how-people-around-the-world-see-democracy-in-8-charts/

de la Torre, C. (2017). Trump's populism: Lessons from Latin America. *Postcolonial Studies, 20*(2), 187–198.

Dimock, M. (2019, June 5). An update on our research unto trust, facts and democracy. *Pew Research Center.* https://www.pewresearch.org/2019/06/05/an-update-on-our-research-into-trust-facts-and-democracy/

Edelman. (2019). *2019 Edelman Trust Barometer.* https://www.edelman.com/sites/g/files/aatuss191/files/2019-02/2019_Edelman_Trust_Barometer_Global_Report.pdf

Edelman. (2020). *2020 Edelman Trust Barometer.* https://www.edelman.com/trust/2020-trust-barometer

Edelman. (2021a). *2021 Edelman Trust Barometer.* https://www.edelman.com/trust/2021-trust-barometer

Edelman. (2021b). *2021 Edelman Trust Barometer Press Release.* https://www.edelman.com/trust/2021-trust-barometer/press-release

Edelman. (2021c). *Trust.* https://www.edelman.com/trust

Esposito, E., Sini, S., & Castagneto, M. (2018). *Roman Jakobson, linguistica e poetica.* Ledizioni.

Fairclough, N. (2003). *Analyzing discourse. Textual analysis for social research.* Routledge.

Former QAnon supporter to Cooper: I apologize for thinking you ate babies. (2021, January 30). *CNN.* https://edition.cnn.com/videos/us/2021/01/30/anderson-cooper-former-qanon-supporter-special-report-sot-ac360-vpx.cnn

Foucault, M. (1972). *The archeology of knowledge and the discourse on language.* Pantheon.

Freedom House. (2018). *Democracy in crisis.* https://freedomhouse.org/report/freedom-world/freedom-world-2018

Freedom House. (2019). *Democracy in retreat. Freedom in the world 2019.* https://freedomhouse.org/sites/default/files/Feb2019_FH_FITW_2019_Report_ForWeb-compressed.pdf

Freedom House. (n.d.). *Our history.* https://freedomhouse.org/about-us/our-history

Freire, P. (1970). *Pedagogy of the oppressed.* Herder & Herder.

Gamson, W. A. (1968). *Power and discontent.* Dorsey.

Global democracy has another bad year. (2020, January 22). *The Economist.* https://www.economist.com/graphic-detail/2020/01/22/global-democracy-has-another-bad-year

Gramsci, A. (1971). *Selections from the prison notebooks of Antonio Gramsci* (Q. Hoare & G. Nowell, Eds. & Trans). International.

Hains, T. (2021). Luntz: Cable News has become a "disaster," only "preaching to the choir" And frankly, I'm disgusted. *Real Clear Politics.* https://www.realclearpolitics.com/video/2021/01/24/frank_luntz_cable_news_is_a_disaster_msnbc_cnn_fox_news_only_preaching_to_the_choir.html

Hariman, R. (1995). *Political style. The artistry of power.* University of Chicago Press.

Hariman, R. (2007). In defense of Jon Stewart. *Critical Studies in Media Communication, 24*(3), 273–277.

Harwell, D., Stanley-Becker, I., Nakhlawi, R., & Timberg, C. (2021, January 14). QAnon reshaped Trump's party and radicalized believers. The Capitol siege may just be the start. *The Washington Post.* https://www.washingtonpost.com/technology/2021/01/13/qanon-capitol-siege-trump/

Hellinger, D. (2019, February 7). Venezuela crisis explained: A tale of two presidents. *The Conversation.* https://theconversation.com/venezuela-crisis-explained-a-tale-of-two-presidents-111198

Hofstadter, R. (2008). *The paranoid style in American politics.* Vintage Books.

Human Rights Watch. (2008a). *A decade under Chávez. Political intolerance and lost opportunities for advancing human rights in Venezuela.* https://www.hrw.org/sites/default/files/reports/venezuela0908web.pdf

Human Rights Watch. (2008b). *Venezuela: Rights suffer under Chavez.* https://www.hrw.org/news/2008/09/18/venezuela-rights-suffer-under-chavez

Human Rights Watch. (2012). *Concentración y abuso de poder en la Venezuela Chávez.* https://www.hrw.org/es/report/2012/07/17/concentracion-y-abuso-de-poder-en-la-venezuela-de-chavez

IDEA. (2019). *The global state of democracy 2019. Addressing the ills, reviving the promise.* https://www.idea.int/sites/default/files/publications/the-global-state-of-democracy-2019.pdf

Information Commissioner's Office. (2018). *Democracy Disputed?* https://ico.org.uk/media/action-weve-taken/2259369/democracy-disrupted-110718.pdf

Jurkowitz, M., Mitchell, A., Shearer, E., & Walker, M. (2020, January 24). 2. Americans are divided by party in the sources they turn to for political news. *Pew Research Center.* https://www.journalism.org/2020/01/24/americans-are-divided-by-party-in-the-sources-they-turn-to-for-political-news/

Jurkowitz, M. (2021, January 11). Republican who relied on trump for news more concerned than other Republicans about election fraud. *Pew Research Center.* https://www.pewresearch.org/fact-tank/2021/01/11/republicans-who-relied-on-trump-for-news-more-concerned-than-other-republicans-about-election-fraud/

Kekic, L. (2007). The Economist Intelligence Unit's index of democracy. *The Economist.* https://www.economist.com/media/pdf/democracy_index_2007_v3.pdf

Latouche, M. A. (2017, May 18). Venezuela has a fake news problem too. *The Conversation.* https://theconversation.com/venezuela-has-a-fake-news-problem-too-77842

Lewis, P., Barr, C., Clarke, S., Voce, A., Levett, C., & Gutiérrez, P. (2019, March 7). Revealed: The rise and rise of populist rhetoric. *The Guardian.* https://www.theguardian.com/world/ng-interactive/2019/mar/06/revealed-the-rise-and-rise-of-populist-rhetoric

Lopez, M. (2019, November 6). Feliz Seijas: Oposición conserva 57, 9% de la intención de voto en futuras elecciones. *Efecto Cocuyo.* https://efectococuyo.com/politica/felix-seijas-oposicion-conserva-579-de-la-intencion-de-voto-en-futuras-elecciones/

Lynch, D. (1992). *Caudillos in Spanish America, 1800–1850.* Clarendon Press, in Questia Online, www.questia.com

Martínez, E. (2018, April 4) Qué dicen las encuestas sobre la situación política en Venezuela? *Prodavinci.* https://prodavinci.com/que-dicen-las-encuestas-sobre-la-situacion-politica-en-venezuela/

Mogelson, L. (2021a, January 17). A reporter's footage from inside the Capitol siege. *The New Yorker.* https://www.newyorker.com/news/video-dept/a-reporters-footage-from-inside-the-capitol-siege

Mogelson, L. (2021b, January 25). Among the insurrectionists. *The New Yorker.* https://www.newyorker.com/magazine/2021/01/25/among-the-insurrectionists

Naylor, B. (2021, January 11). Impeachment resolution cites Trump's 'incitement' of Capitol insurrection. *NPR.* https://www.npr.org/sections/trump-impeachment-effort-live-updates/2021/01/11/955631105/impeachment-resolution-cites-trumps-incitement-of-capitol-insurrection

Negrine, R., & Papathanassopoulos, S. (2011). The transformation of political communication. In S. Papathanassopoulos (Ed.), *Media perspectives for the 21st century* (pp. 41–54). Routledge.

Newman, N. (2020). Executive summary and key findings of the 2020 Report. *Reuters; Digital News Report.* https://www.digitalnewsreport.org/survey/2020/overview-key-findings-2020/

Norris, P., & Inglehart, R. (2019). *Cultural backlash: The rise of authoritarian-populism.* Cambridge University Press.

Pensamiento y Acción (1996). *Cultura democrática en Venezuela. Informe analítico de los resultados de una encuesta de opinión publica.* Fundación Pensamiento y Acción.

Pfetsch, B. (2004). From political culture to political communications culture: A theoretical approach to comparative analysis. In F. Esser, & B. Pfetsch (Eds.), *Comparing political communication: Theories, cases and challenges* (pp. 344–366). Cambridge University Press.

Putnam, R. D., Leonardi, R., & Nanetti, R. (1993). *Making democracy work: Civic traditions in modern Italy.* Princeton University Press.

Ramos Avalos, J. (2007). *Las tres mentiras de Hugo Chávez.* Jorge Ramos. https://jorgeramos.com/las-tres-mentiras-de-hugo-chavez/

Repucci, S., & Slipowitz, A., (2020, October 19). Democracy under lockdown. *Freedom House.* https://freedomhouse.org/sites/default/files/2020-10/COVID-19_Special_Report_Final_.pdf

Schenkkan, N. (2020, September 1). Special Coronavirus focus: Venezuela. *Freedom House.* https://freedomhouse.org/article/special-coronavirus-focus-venezuela

Silverstein, M. (2003). *Talking politics: The substance of style from Abe to "W".* Prickly Paradigm Press.

Tasker, P. (2016). Peter Tasker: The flawed 'Science' behind democracy rankings. *Nikkei Asia.* https://asia.nikkei.com/NAR/Articles/Peter-Tasker-The-flawed-science-behind-democracy-rankings

Taylor, C. (2002). Modern social imaginaries. *Public Culture, 14*(1), 91–124.

The Heritage Foundation. (2018, February 16). *Freedom House turns partisan.* https://www.heritage.org/global-politics/commentary/freedom-house-turns-partisan

Thompson, G. (2020). *Post-truth public relations: Communication in an era of digital disinformation* (1st ed.). Routledge

Tight Shot. (2021, January 24). Trump Supporters denounce media. *Fox News.* https://video.foxnews.com/v/6225793665001#sp=show-clips

Trump, D. (2021, 6 January). Donald Trump Speech "Save America" Rally Transcript January 6. *Rev.* https://www.rev.com/blog/transcripts/donald-trump-speech-save-america-rally-transcript-january-6

Van Aelst, P., Strömbäck, J., Aalberg, T., Esser, F., de Vreese, C., Matthes, J., Hopmann, D., Salgado, S., Hubé, N., Stępińska, A., Papathanassopoulos, S., Berganza, R., Legnante, G., Reinemann, C., Sheafer, T., & Stanyer, J. (2017). Political communication in a high-choice media environment: A challenge for democracy? *Annals of the International Communication Association, 41*(1), 3–27. https://doi.org/10.1080/23808985.2017.1288551

Van Dijk, T. A. (1997). What is political discourse analysis? *Belgian Journal of Linguistics, 11*(1), 11–52.

Voltmer, K. (Ed.) (2006). *Mass media and political communication in new democracies.* Routledge.

Waisbord, S. (2018). Why populism and troubling for democratic communication. *Communication, Culture and Critique, 11*(1), 21–34.

Warner, J. (2007). Political culture jamming: The dissident humor of "The daily show with Jon Stewart". *Popular Communication, 5*(1), 17–36.

Wike, R., Silver, L., & Castillo, A. (2019, April 29). Many across the globe are dissatisfied with how democracy is working. *Pew Research Center.* https://www.pewresearch.org/global/2019/04/29/many-across-the-globe-are-dissatisfied-with-how-democracy-is-working/

Wodak, R. (2015). *The politics of fear. What right-wing populist discourses mean.* Sage.

Young, I. M. (1997). Difference as a Resource for democratic communication. In J. Bohman & W. Rehg (Eds.), *Deliberative democracy: Essays on reason and politics* (pp. 383–404). MIT Press. https://ebookcentral-proquest-com.ezproxy.library.uq.edu.au

3 Populist communication, discursive violence, and disrupted democracy

In this chapter, I build the theoretical architecture that underpins and shapes the discursive disruption framework. I discuss three core theoretical themes: Authoritarian populist communication; modern discourses of democracy; and the concept of discursive disruption. I illustrate these themes with examples from my two case studies, Venezuela's late President Hugo Chávez and the United States' (US) President Donald Trump. Discursive disruption is thus represented as a multilevel concept that encompasses theoretical and analytical components that are aimed to aid in the identification, analysis, and understanding of disruptions in the discourses of democracy.

I started this book with the following puzzle: Populist rhetoric has been rising and democratic discourses have been declining or disrupted. Is there a connection between these two themes?

To answer this question, the first theoretical task is to review and situate theories of authoritarian populism and populist communication.

3.1 Authoritarian populist communication

As suggested in earlier chapters, although I do take the ideological angle into account, I do not approach populism as an ideology focused on studying right-wing nativist parties or politicians (see for example, the work of Mudde & Rovira Kaltwasser, 2018). And although I include antagonism as one of the main features of the populist talk, I do not interpret populism as a phenomenon that is solely based on Manichaean appeals (see Hawkins, 2010). Populist communicators also use emotional and patriotic appeals that are embedded in, and nurture, citizens' already existing frustrations and disenchantments with democracy, politics, and government; frustrations and disenchantments that are complex, not always or solely Manichean, and can vary depending on cultures, contexts, and

DOI: 10.4324/9781003118602-3

times. Drawing on Williams's (1977) structures of feeling, I argue that populism suggests feelings, emotions, and beliefs continuously emerging and reemerging from and within democracy that should be considered as indicators implying that something is not working in the system. I also argue that there are groups of unhappy or alienated citizens that are liable to be attracted by the irrational, antidialogic, populist talk. Although frustrated or disenfranchised, most of the citizens that identify with populist leaders are also part of their respective countries, and, hence, should be included in the democratic conversation instead of being viewed as a threat, outsiders or *deplorables*, the unfortunate term used by Hillary Clinton to refer to Trump's supporters (Blair, 2017).

One of the main strengths of populist communicators is that they know how to connect with people who may feel confused or fearful of change in their ways of life. For example, depending on the political or socioeconomic situation and his popularity in the polls, Chávez strategically chose to use positive appeals (enthusiasm, sympathy, or pride) or negative appeals (fear, anger, or anxiety) in his speeches to connect with different audiences and pursue some of his policy aims (Escalante-Block, 2018). Also, most populist leaders aim to bond with their populist audiences through monolithic nationalistic arguments, which Ernst et al. (2019) called "absolutism", that is, the patriotic sentiments through which populist players stress "the superiority of own country by referencing an idealized and utopic heartland" (p. 4), exemplified by Trump's Make America Great Again (MAGA) discourse and Chávez's Bolivarianism. Orly Kayam (2018), for example, argued that Trump styled himself as an antipolitical outsider by decrying political conventions and democratic rules, a leader destined to return the US to "its former greatness" (p. 183). For Kayam (2018), Trump's language typifies the ultimate "Anti-Political Rhetorical Strategy" (p. 202), characterized by the use of emotional appeals such as *"negativity, simplicity, repetition and hyperbole* [emphasis added]*"* (p. 183). Both Chávez and Trump talked to their politically alienated bases through emotional appeals that enabled them not only to connect but also to bond with them, continuously transforming political events or issues into emotional episodes.

Notably, Norris and Inglehart's (2019) defined authoritarian populism as a philosophy and style of politics that promotes nationalism, conservative morals, and anti-multiculturalism. Norris (2016) argued elsewhere that the surge of populist authoritarianism "can best be explained as a cultural backlash in Western societies against long-term, ongoing social change" (para. 18). Supported by the World

Values Survey, Norris (2016) suggested that many Western societies have become more liberal on many social issues, which has represented a threat to traditional values and ways of life. However, Norris (2016) added that among the younger generations there is an increasing preference for authoritarian leaders that do not want to be accountable to elections or congress, as 44% of noncollege graduates view positively having "a strong leader unchecked by elections and Congress" (para. 24). This analysis is consistent with the results of the 38-nation study delivered by the Pew Research Centre in 2017, which suggested that although in more than half in each of the studied nations, there is ample support for both representative and direct democracy, still "many endorse nondemocratic alternatives" (p. 1). These results imply that there is both (a) an attraction toward authoritarian leaders, and (b) a "shallow commitment" to representative/liberal democratic forms of government, even in advanced industrialized countries. Specifically, the same Pew Research Centre's (2017) study indicated that in 20 countries, "a quarter or more of those polled think a system in which a strong leader can make decisions without interference from parliament, or the courts is a good form of government" (p. 4). These results explain in part the rise of authoritarian populist leaders and the success of their themes (e.g., Brexit) in Western democratic countries.

The preference for authoritarian leaders might seem a novelty in the US and other Western countries but this trend is not new in Latin America. Cultural imaginaries associated with the authoritarian figure of the *caudillo* have dominated Latin American political culture for decades (Caballero, 2010; Pino-Iturrieta, 2006). In the case of Venezuela, historian Elias Pino-Iturrieta (2006) argued that the country is in a permanent search for a "providential man", following the myth of the "strong good man" (p. 269). In the same vein, Welsch et al. (2004), in a comparative analysis about Venezuelan political culture using data from the World Values Survey of 1996 and 2000, confirmed that although the majority of Venezuelans considered democracy as "the best" type of government, respondents paradoxically gave high, and even equal, value to the ideas of "freedom", "order", and of having a "strong man" in government (p. 65); Venezuelans wanted democracy as long as it was accompanied by "authority and firmness" (p. 65).

Levitsky and Loxton (2013), for example, used of the concept of "competitive authoritarianism" to examine contemporary Latin American populist rulers such as Chávez in Venezuela, Evo Morales in Bolivia and Rafael Correa in Ecuador. They argued that the disappearance of military dictatorships has not led to either the complete obliteration of authoritarianism, or the emergence of stable and durable democracies

in the region; they argued that, "fragile democracies slid into competitive authoritarianism or electoral regimes in which widespread incum-
bency abuse skewed the playing field against opponents" (Levitsky &
Loxton, 2013, p. 107). Populist players mobilize popular support by
using (a) emotional appeals that are mainly negative and antiestablishment, (b) their character as antipolitical outsiders or mavericks, and
(c) the personal relation they build with their voters, mainly through
bypassing political and party institutions. Levitsky and Loxton (2013)
added that authoritarian populist leaders, who are elected and act
within democracy, tend to act as "elected autocrats" with the power to
reshape the system from within.

In this light, some academics but especially news media commentators have developed arguments about the lessons that Western countries,
especially the US, should learn from the Latin American experiences.
For example, writer and academic Diego von Vacano (2019) represented
Donald Trump as an "American caudillo" that used "princely performative" forms of populism that have been attributed to Latin-American
populist par excellence, Juan Domingo Peron. Trump was also called
"*el caudillo yanqui*" by *The Washington Post* editorialist Ishaan Tharoor
(2017, para. 2), who argued that Latin American immigrants in the US,
who have lived under populist regimes, felt like Trump "has been taking
notes" (para. 8) from military despots in their countries. As Figure 3.1
illustrates, this idea has already been represented by Venezuelan
visual artist Eduardo Sanabria's (@EDOIlustrado) cartoon "Populism
for Dummies".

3.1.1 The communicative, mediatic, and audience dimensions of populism

There is a critical aspect, key to understanding populism and the disruptions it may cause, that sometimes gets neglected or minimized,
which consists of the *communicative*, *media*, and *audience* dimensions
of the populist process. Authoritarian populist players display a rather
contradictory use of communication and media. Populist players tend
to reject and bypass news media or journalistic scrutiny but, at the same
time, they have demonstrated that they are skillful users of mediatic and
nonmediatic venues, outlets and platforms that enable them to communicate *directly* with their followers, constituents, or audiences. Populists
employ likeminded or partisan news media outlets and social media
platforms, as well as face-to-face meetings and rallies to build a direct
link and bond with their audiences. Populists tend to view and represent mainstream or elite media outlets and journalism as "the enemy"

Figure 3.1 "Populism for Dummies" (2016)

Source: Courtesy of visual artist Eduardo Sanabria (EDO Ilustrado)

and their reports as "fake news", but, paradoxically, they also aim to be covered by those same journalists, a trait shared by both right- and left-wing populists. Thus, populist leaders' appeal and success also depend on the communication channels they use, and the extent to which their emotional and antipolitical rhetoric turns controversial or disruptive enough to both mobilize their politically disenchanted audiences and become newsworthy enough to dominate the agenda, even, or especially because, they are a constant source of journalistic criticism. Therefore, *authoritarian populists feed off emotional and mediatic controversy, even, or especially, when the news media criticize, mock, or condemn them.* The victimization boosted by mediatic attacks makes populist leaders even more appealing to their bases.

The communicative dimension of populism was first studied by scholars such as Waisbord (2003) and Jagers and Walgrave (2007), who defined populism as a political communication style. Jagers and Walgrave (2007) conceptualized populism as "a political communication style of political actors that refers to the people" (p. 322). Later, Aalberg et al. (2017) explained populism "as a set of features or elements of communicative messages that have their roots in—or resonate with—the goals, motives, and attitudes of political actors, the media, or citizens" (p. 14). Ernst et al. (2019) proposed an all-inclusive concept of populist communication that defined it as "the representation of the populist ideology (what is being said) and the use of populism-related stylistic elements (how something is being said) by all sorts of political actors" (p. 2). Although this last definition seems to separate populist messages and style, the authors later used Kriesi (2018) to argue that "populist content and populist style tend to go together" (p. 13), which is consistent with Silverstein's (2003) idea discussed in Chapter 1, that the "message strategically deploys style" (p. 15). Therefore, *in populist communication, style and message are not just intertwined, but one and the same.*

3.1.2 Audience populism, hate speech, and cancel culture

What is audience populism? Hameleers (2019) incorporated the role of "populist audiences" to the populism-democracy interplay, by arguing that the way some citizens construct divisive, hostile, nationalist messages on online communities "maybe harmful for deliberative democracy" (p. 147). Although online platforms are not representative of public opinion, audience engagement, messages, and style of communication have the potential to "outweigh" pluralism, diversity, and truth by "identity-based coverage" (Hameleers, 2019, p. 147). Hameleers (2019) also stressed how "boundary constructions are central in populist identity discourse" (pp. 149–150). Put simply, *in the same way that populist leaders and audiences strategize or weaponize words, they can also strategize and weaponize identity,* which proves that identity politics is a critical element of the populist talk.

For example, two different but equally extreme and polarizing audience practices associated with identity, such as hate speech and cancel culture, involve discursive practices that have had reputational and legal consequence in the offline realm. Although they are ideologically opposed, they are similar in their communicative style: Both are audience speech practices that *mirror* the antidialogic, antagonistic, emotional, and insulting communication style of populist leaders such as Hugo Chávez and Donald Trump. "Hate speech", often associated with ultranationalists and bigots, has been defined as the vilification, abuse, and discrimination of minority and marginalized groups

(Banks, 2010; Gelber, 2011; Howard, 2020). "Cancel culture", more associated with extreme progressives, has been defined by Bouvier (2020) and Norris (2020) as shaming, ostracizing, and boycotting individuals or groups based on moral, usually social justice, grounds.

Both, hate speech and cancel culture practitioners use freedom of expression conventions as an all-inclusive protective flag that gives them the right to shun or obliterate others. However, paradoxically, both disregard the law by taking justice into their own hands, into their own voices, and into their own social media posts, thumbing their noses at norms and conventions in the same fashion that populist leaders bypass separation of powers and feel free to bully opponents.

Cancel culture and hate speech performers' tactics include the use of powerful, abrasive, and divisive words, keywords and hashtags that not only boost outrage, but also trigger social and political disruptions, which ultimately might, either with or without intention, close the political dialogue, and lead to political communication shutdowns. And, in the same way populists use democracy to rise to power and disrupt and reshape democracy from within, cancel culture and hate speech agents shield behind their democratic rights and the invisibility provided by social media platforms. Ultimately, through their cancelling communicative practices these operators consciously or unconsciously put the same free speech they use and abuse "under threat".

An open letter signed by 150 academics, published initially by *Harper's Magazine*, noted that while the signatories recognized that social justice protests and demands for police reform, equality, and inclusion were not only needed but long overdue. The academics also showed concerns about the tone of the response, indicating that "this needed reckoning has also intensified a new set of moral attitudes and political commitments that tend to weaken our norms of open debate and toleration of differences in favor of ideological conformity" ("A Letter on Justice and Open Debate", 2020, para. 1). While the signatories of the letter condemned Trump as a champion of exclusion and a threat to democracy, they stressed that the answer is not a resistance that is "allowed to harden into its own brand of dogma or coercion" ("A Letter on Justice and Open Debate", 2020, para. 1); they also made a strong argument that directly pointed to the dangers that arise from the discursive disruption logic proposed by this book indicating, "the democratic inclusion we want can be achieved only if we speak out against the intolerant climate that has set in on all sides" (para. 1). In other words, the solution or response to hate and cancel culture, or to disruptive populist discourses, should not be shaped by newer brands of even more dogmatic, intolerant, disruptive, and coercive hate or cancel politics.

3.1.3 Populist media

The use of populist communication tools is not restricted to politicians and audiences: News media outlets and journalists moderate, circulate, and in some cases also use populist rhetoric, as *The Guardian's* study on the rise of populist rhetoric reviewed in Chapters 1 and 2 also demonstrated (Lewis et al., 2019). News media and journalism employ populist communication strategies and tactics not only to appeal to their audiences but also, of course, to profit; hence the idea of "media populism", which is populism "among the media themselves" (Krämer, 2014, p. 42).

Media outlets and platforms use a populist style of communication without being necessarily attached to a party. Tabloids and talk shows are representative of various forms of media populism (by displaying emotionalized, patriotic, or antipolitical kinds of talk) that appeal to populist audiences. Recent research shows that online communities, mainly Facebook and Twitter, are also significant vehicles of both media and audience populism (Bracciale & Martella, 2017; Ernst et al., 2019; Hameleers, 2019; Mazzoleni & Bracciale, 2018; Postill, 2018). As Postill (2018) argued, populist agents (leaders, audiences, media) have been skillful users of media outlets and platforms at their disposal in different contexts and times.

3.1.4 The populist communication style

To end this section, I use my own work with emeritus professor Ralph Negrine (Block & Negrine, 2017) that reviewed and categorized the main traits of the populist communication style. After a careful review of the literature, and also based on our original research, we identified three key strategies: Adversarial language, identity politics, and use of and relationship with the media. For the purposes of this book, I have complemented and updated some of the variables in Block and Negrine's (2017) framework, mainly associated with new data about populist players, stressing the use of affects and emotions in populist communication, and changes prompted and offered by digital and social media affordances, as follows:

a   Adversarial language: Populism has a communicative essence and emotional style. *Populist acts are primarily discursive acts.* Emotional, antagonistic, antidialogic, and impolite discursive or speech acts are crucial stylistic tools used by populist players (Block & Negrine, 2017; Bolivar, 2018; Hawkins, 2010; Moffitt

& Tormey, 2014). They are affective and emotional because, as Papacharissi (2021) argued, affects are used as intensity tools that trigger emotions and feelings in specific settings and times. Populist leaders, often fetishized as some sort of pseudo-messiahs "connect affectively" as they "present that mix of 'facts' drama, opinion and intensity blended into one" (Papacharissi, 2021, p. 131). Populist players captivate both their audiences and journalists alike as they are "enamored" with a style that triggers strong emotions. Emotions that, I argue, lead to bonding and mimetization among the likeminded but also exclusion of "the Other", and deep antidialogic divides and disruptions in the polity. In news media environments, such emotions lead to sensationalistic coverage, news recirculation, ratings, sharing, retweets, clickbaits, and profit.

b   Identity politics: Populists are identity politics operators. One of the classic characteristics attributed to populists is the way they strategize their appeal to *the people* (Canovan, 1999: Jagers & Walgrave, 2007), and the way they construct such people in terms of antipolitical frustrations, fear, and resentment; a collective actor that usually is represented as the disenfranchised, the forgotten, the individuals, and groups unsatisfied or unhappy with establishment politics and democracy or the way democracy is run by the elites (Laclau, 2005). Thus, identity and appeal to the people are socially and *communicatively* constructed. Populist leaders also build the people in patriotic, nationalistic ways, propelling their views through moral language claiming the primacy of their nation and/or ethnicity. Populists construct a collective actor united by similar needs, aspirations, unsatisfied demands and expectations, or frustrations vis-à-vis the existing or former ruling elites (Laclau, 2005).

c   Use of the media: The third populist strategy encompasses the peculiar way populists engage with the news and social media; a topic already introduced in the previous section. On the one hand, populist politicians build confrontational relationships with journalists and editors representing them as "the enemy"; on the other hand, populist players are savvy news and social media operators. The ongoing mediatic controversy has helped populists put their messages across, even when they are fiercely criticized, as they obtain prevalent places in, and even manage to dominate, the political agenda. Mazzoleni (2003) argued that contemporary populist actors have relied "on some kind of indirect (and direct) complicity with the mass media and all are led by politicians who, with few exceptions, are shrews and capable 'news makers' themselves" (p. 6). Mazzoleni (2003) added that "media action is ineluctably embroiled" (p. 6) in the rise and development of populism; populist players usually "defy" the elites and attempt to disrupt political systems with "their abrasive language, public protests, and emotive issues" (p, 7), and the coverage of these issues "may amount to unintentional yet concrete support for populist actions" (p. 7). In the digital age, populism continues to make savvy use of platform media. As Vaccari and Valeriani (2018) suggested, platform media and politics have increased political mobilization and participation as citizens can identify swiftly and easily with clear-cut positions, often represented by the abrasive and extremist populist talk. Populist leaders and parties are savvy users of all types of media, especially social media platforms, which they even prefer over old-fashioned talk shows (Ernst et al., 2019).

Based on the updated and adjusted version of Block and Negrine's (2017) definition, I describe populism as an antidialogic and monologic (hence antidemocratic) political communication style that effectively and affectively uses language, identity politics, and a savvy yet confrontational use of media to connect, mobilize, and bond with its audiences—the people, the sovereign yet disenfranchised populist voters. An antagonistic communication style that also, and simultaneously, focuses on alienating and dividing opponents. As I suggested in Chapter 2, *populist language embodies discursive violence committed on democratic political communication*, an argument that I intend to demonstrate throughout this study.

3.2 Western democratic discourses

I approach democracy from a critical and discursive political communication perspective. I examine the discourses of modern democracy as one of the fundamental pillars of the theoretical architecture that supports the discursive disruption framework. In this section I complement some of the ideas already situated in Chapter 1, where I used Farrelly's (2015) categorization of democracy: (a) liberal or "legal", (b) representative (either "competitive elitist" or "classic pluralist"), and (c) participatory, deliberative, "discursive", and *communicative* democracy. For its relevance to my argument on discursive disruption, I specifically expand on Young's (1997a) communicative democracy.

Although each one of these categories embodies different worldviews and approaches to democracy, they share two common principles:

Democracy is a system that is, or should be, about *the rule of the people*, and the people's "sovereign" ethos. The idea of sovereignty, the "artificiall[sic] soul" that "gives life and motion" (Hobbes, 2015, p. 44) to the whole body of the state, is represented by the frontispiece of the Leviathan. Narratives evoking the people and the sovereign nation are central to democratic constitutions and are also fundamental to populist manifestos. The difference lies in the way populist leaders employ these terms, the people and sovereignty, as arguments against democracy itself.

The discourses of the sovereignty of the people, which evolved during the French Revolution by the hand of Abbé Sieyès (Sonenscher, 2003), who was one the main drafters of the *Declaration of the Rights of Man and of the Citizen*, and the idea of identifying or naming the unprivileged people as the "Third Estate". Enlightenment narratives have been central to both, democratic and populist discourses that exacerbate the virtue of the sovereign people; a construction that is particularly used by populist leaders to convey the supremacy of the "*descamisados*, workers, peasants, small entrepreneurs, indigenous groups, and marginal populations" (Worsley, 1969, p. 242). Terms like sovereignty and the people are constructs that can be adjusted by political, and, especially, populist leaders to appeal to the interests, expectations, frustrations and fears of specific audiences, especially populist audiences, to create their own imaginaries of the popular will (both Chávez's Bolivarian and Trump's MAGA peoples are just two examples).

For example, in Venezuela the term sovereignty became *untransferable* [emphasis added] in the chavista constitution sanctioned in 1999, which ensured that "the organs of the state emanated from popular sovereignty, and they are subject to it" ("Constitución de la República", 1999). This approach to the sovereignty of the Bolivarian people was repeatedly used by Chávez and his successors to validate their words and acts against the separation of powers and also, as a weapon to attack opposing parties and news media that they represented as the enemies of the *sovereign people*. Donald Trump also used the argument of people's sovereignty mainly in his MAGA speeches delivered domestically and internationally.

3.2.1 A discursive and communicative approach to democracy

I will expand now on some of the ideas about democracy introduced in Chapter 1 and also add other views that are helpful to explain some of the variables and indicators, but also the tensions associated with the concept. For example, Habermas's (1984) views of "communicative action" and especially the idea of the *public sphere* are often employed in discussions about democracy. Communicative action describes dialogic interactions "without reservations", which for Habermas (1984) were morally superior because they lacked partisan strategic intentions as their main goal is, or should be, reaching understanding. The public sphere has been loosely used as a sort of shorthand for democracy. Although the public sphere has been helpful to idealistically describe common spaces for communication and democratic performance, it has been criticized precisely for its idealism in assuming that everybody can communicate on equal terms and without any strategic aims: Real life political communication interactions are strategic, often uncivil and, importantly, not always aimed at understanding but at dialogue and debate, which are at the heart of political discourse. Also, there is not one, but multiple public spheres that are specific to their own contexts, cultures, participants, and times. To achieve their political goals, humans use *strategic* communication, that is, communication with a purpose or intention by employing communicative tactics and tools to build and maintain relationships and a desired outcome associated with the pursuance of power and (ideally) the common good. Therefore, the emergence of problems and conflicts over power and resources in society should be anticipated and acknowledged, not muted or obliterated by always assuming the possibility of consensus or understanding.

A working concept of democracy for the purposes of this book should include not only normative and idealistic Western indicators of modern democracy (i.e., separation of power, rule of law, free and fair elections, respect for freedoms and rights; political and economic accountability) but also possibilities of plural dialogue and debate, understanding and conflict, as well as the disruptions triggered by everyday democratic and communicative practices in power relations. At the heart of truly democratic discourses lies plural and reflective communication and contestation; communication that includes but exceeds just the regular performance of free and fair elections.

After the senate did not get the 67 votes needed to impeach Donald Trump, President Joe Biden ("Trump Impeachment Trial", 2021) asserted that this episode had reminded American citizens, and probably the world watching the impeachment drama, that "democracy is fragile" and "must always be defended" (para. 11), and that we must always be alert about extreme and intolerant discourses that continuously challenge the system.

I take a critical, communicative, *discursive,* approach to democracy, to identify and study those challenges, especially because there is not a single but many discourses and representations of democracy, and the dominant views are predominantly normative, idealistic, and unavoidably Americanized. Often these views do not consider power unbalances, the ever-present possibility of conflict, and irrational events that also can disturb or change democracy. A classic example is the idealistic approach to democracy promoted by Almond and Verba's (1965) "civic culture" centered on values of stability, equilibrium, level of *civic-ness,* separation of powers, and social order. Conversely, Pateman (1970) provided a critique that represented democracy as the "set of institutional arrangements at national level" (p. 14), where the main but rather insufficient event is "the competition of leaders (elites) for the votes of the people at periodic, free elections" (p. 14). Also from a critical perspective, Young (2000) explained that there are certain values that are shared by two of the main approaches to modern democracy, namely, deliberative/aggregative and representative, such as "a rule of law, that voting is the means of making decisions when consensus is not possible or too costly to achieve, that democratic process requires freedom of speech, assembly, association and so on" (p. 18). However, Young (1997a) stressed the importance of *communication, dialogue,* and *contestation* in *plural* environments as the basis of any discourse that aims to be called *democratic.*

But it is precisely the permanent challenge to communication, contestation, and plurality that populist players bring to the public conversation—their craving for *totality*—that leads to democratic disruptions and dysfunctions. Thus, I argue that populist communication, that antidialogic/monologic communicative style that is so appealing to some politically disenchanted groups, is the opposite to communicative or discursive types of democracy.

As Papacharissi (2021) suggested, "democracy is a fixed ideal with flexible morphology" (p. 60). Contemporary democratic ideals use terms like freedom, equality, justice, globalism, citizen participation or voice that in practice, depending on contexts and times, might mean different things, or involve contradictory interpretations. The tensions that arise between the exercise of duties and rights, freedoms and equality, justice and voice, patriotism and globalism can be challenging, leading to changes that can be positive to society and democracy, but also to conflicts that can lead to dialogue blockage and closure. These tensions have also pushed changes in the pre-existing "morphologies" of democracy in some countries, like what happened in Venezuela with the change of the 1961 representative democracy constitution, to the 1999 participatory democracy constitution, where terms such as *representation, participation,* and *people's sovereignty* were reshaped or rebranded, by Chávez and his clique in the construction of power and identity.

3.2.2 The discourses of democracy

Now, why does this book use the term *discourse* or rather *discourses* to describe or define democracy? I use the term *discourse* broadly, borrowing from Foucault's (1972) "discursive formations," to describe a series of regular statements embodying a set of languages, routines, rules, protocols, and practices that include both dialogue and debate, that have been normalized and naturalized in specific groups or societies. Therefore, and probably controversially for some, I also draw on Foucault (1972) to suggest that democracy is a discourse, or a set of discourses constructed across history, societies, and circumstances. Democracy in all its forms, modern or ancient, embodies different shapes or "morphologies" in the one term. Western, modern, or conventional democratic discourses have loosely referred to systems of government that in one way or another have guaranteed free and fair elections, rule of law, separation of powers, and other democratic freedoms, rights and duties. In this context, the concept of discursive disruption aims to help identify, analyze, and understand the process or logic triggering disruptions in such "fostered" democratic discourses, and their conventions and norms of interaction, in specific groups or societies.

The discourses of democracy and republicanism are rooted in the thought of rational and skeptical thinkers from the Enlightenment, who promoted individual liberties against authoritarian rulers and institutions. However, it is important to note here that republicanism is linked but not equal to democracy. While republicanism promoted the idea of representation and the rule of the educated political elite, democracy used to be regarded as a dangerous form of government until the middle of the 19th century, because it could lead to what de Tocqueville (2003) classically called the "tyranny of the majority", the rule of the mob.

In his analysis of Machiavelli's view of princes and the art of the state, Viroli (1993), suggested "Liberty can be sustained only through virtue and conflict" (p.160) in the pursuit of the common good, of the *vivere politico*, where humans flourish and achieve happiness and "civil equality". Viroli (1993) explained that for the Florentine, the prince (or leader) must be temperate, constant, prudent, and just as, for him, "fortitude ... without prudence turns into temerity" (p. 165), "prudence without justice becomes craftiness... or malice" (p. 165), and, importantly, "justice without temperance becomes cruelty" (p. 165). And, as Viroli (1993) noted, "Machiavelli did not reject the republican concept of politics and the political man. Rather he reworked the vocabulary of civil philosophy to make it useful in a new political context" (p. 171).

After the Enlightenment, the discourses of democracy evolved, on the one hand, through Kantian/Habermasian ideals of building a reasoned dialogue and "the agreement of free citizens" (O'Neill, 2002, p. 249); and, on the other, through radical democratic views claiming that all humans have "the same right to pursue happiness and think and say whatever they see fit" (Israel, 2009, p. 54). The 20th century put democracy in a new light as "odious connotations...gradually receded" (Hanson, 1989, p. 68), and it became instead the dominant or hegemonic symbol of popular sovereignty, justice, and equality.

Thus, unresolved ideological tensions embedded in idealistic views of democracy, especially due to contradictory conceptions of liberty and equality, have obscured the practice of democracy across the years (Castro Leiva, 1999). Such contradictions and tensions, inherited from the 18th century when the French revolution "signaled the emergence of a radical tradition of democracy that was quite distinct from the tradition of liberal democracy in England" (Hanson, 1989, p. 75), were further complicated by Rousseau's exacerbation of the sovereignty of the people and general will narratives, which inspired Simon Bolivar and the emancipation movements in South America. Against this view, the American Founding Fathers preferred republicanism as they saw democracy as a source of turbulence, or disruption. After all, as Hanson (1989) argued, the concept of democracy has had "a rhetorical ascendance" (p. 84), especially in the Americas, which has triggered its numerous interpretations, typologies, and connotations, especially regarding the study of its dysfunctions, imperfections, and disruptions.

Returning to Young's (1997b) definition of democracy, as a "form of practical reason for conflict resolution and collective problem solving" (p. 400), citizens have "a commitment to cooperation and to looking for the most just solution" (p. 400), equivalent to the idea of the common good, "a method for determining the best and most just solution to conflicts and other collective problems" (p. 400). Democratic politics involves taking into account private concerns and common interests together, but also "critical dialogue among the plurality of socially differentiated perspectives present in the social field" (Young, 1997b, p. 401). Young (1997b) understood plurality as the key feature of publicity and the *public*. In this light, Young's (1997b) prerequisites for a democratic dialogue are (a) plurality of perspectives, (b) confrontation between different perspectives where everybody *listens*, and (c) "Expressing, questioning, challenging differently situated knowledge

[that] adds to social knowledge" (p.403). In other words, a true communicative democracy needs debate among well-informed citizens, vivid dialogue, and a sincere aim for resolution.

3.2.3 Shrinking common ground

A special note needs to be added about the role formerly played by the mass media (Norris & Inglehart, 2019), as a common ground where political and media actors promoted democracy and cosmopolitan ways of life, tolerance to others, free markets, liberal sexual morals, advocacy, civism, and civilism. The mass media, or news media, the so called *fourth state* (another elastic construct), has been challenged and diminished economically and politically—as a business model and as the paladin of freedom of expression and keeping power accountable—by the rise of new algorithmically governed models, the fragmentation of digital channels and social media platforms mainly based on click bait, and by the popularity, or *virality* of extreme positions boosting differences instead of commonalities. These digital spaces often promote what separates us, instead of what should unite us as humans. The news media, the former common ground, or idealistic public sphere, has changed dramatically and is continuously adjusting to new formats and platforms in the face of digital disruptions, instability, and "turbulence", triggered, particularly, by how people connect and engage with media platforms in their everyday lives (Yasseri et al., 2016). After all, as Kriesi (2013) suggested, political communication processes and practices depend "on the media infrastructure" and are subject not only to the continuous and dramatic changes suffered by such infrastructure but also to its intrusion into democracy.

Moreover, it is crucial to understand the significance of receding common grounds, of democratic spaces for plural and civil deliberation and its links with discursive disruption. The idea of a common ground was interpreted by Arendt (1998), who argued that "the public realm, as the common world, gathers us together and yet prevents our falling over each other" (p. 52). For Arendt (1998), this common world is a "web of relationships" (p. 183), made of *speech* and *action*, through which humans build together the political stage and insert themselves into the human world. However, Arendt (1998) warned about the possibility of breakages in the realm of public affairs, which she explained in terms of the *in-between*—the by-space between speech and action—that connects and separates men at the same time. Arendt (1998) argued that at the heart of those breakages was an issue of "thoughtlessness", the loss of commonality, the "heedless recklessness or hopeless confusion or complacent repetition of 'truths' which have become trivial and empty" (p. 5).

One illustration about the loss of shared spaces in contemporary democracies is provided by Portland's mayor Ted Wheeler, a Republican, who applied the idea of the "missing middle" to American political discourse: "We need to change our political discourse in this country. It's become very personal, it's become more polarized. The left and the right are moving farther apart. We have a missing middle in our political discourse" (Steinmetz, 2017, June 20).

The missing middle described by mayor Wheeler is often represented by some mainstream politicians and journalists in terms of a shared public reality, or shared media spaces within which audiences can disagree, dispute, and challenge each other. *BBC* reporter and presenter Alan Little ("Fake News & Post Truth", 2016) suggested that democratic societies are losing those shared spaces and that traditional journalism (and I would also add traditional politics) have been superseded and lost a significant part of their communicative power to the Internet and social media platforms that have become the true mediators, moderators, and gatekeepers; there are now multiple realities in which citizens are listening to their own preferred sources which, in Little's ("Fake News & Post Truth", 2016) view is dangerous and damaging democracy.

Another illustration, that nostalgically focuses on the media as the shared or common ground, is provided by former president Barrack Obama in his 2017 speech at the University of Chicago (Rhodan, 2017). Obama explained that until recently everyone used to share the same information through the mass mediated news, but that at the moment:

> Because of changes in the media, we now have a situation in which everybody's listening to people who already agree with them and are further and further reinforcing their own realities to the neglect of a common reality that allows us to have a healthy debate and then try to find common ground and actually move solutions forward.
>
> (Rhodan, 2017, para. 14).

The preoccupation about the media as common ground for political discussion has also been raised by Latin American scholars and commentators, especially about the lack of middle-ground spaces in deeply mediatized and polarized Venezuela, where a clash of confrontational political identities has boosted an ongoing political and socioeconomic deterioration, polarization, and violence. For example, Kitzberger

(2020) argued that the greatest challenge in Venezuela has been to be find "a minimum common ground that allows [us] to recreate a peaceful democratic coexistence. The size of that challenge can be measured by the same difficulty of visualizing its resolution" (para. 1).

Interestingly, Swart et al. (2019) added a key element to the discussion: Although they agreed that "the news has traditionally served as a common ground, enabling people to connect to others and engage with public issues they encounter in everyday life" (p. 902), they also suggested that the issue is not any more about what the news *means* for their audiences, but about how, why, and where audiences *connect*, *understand*, and *negotiate* their engagement with the news and, I would add, with politics.

Political communication and democracy today are more about *what is* meaningful, valuable, and worthwhile for citizens or audiences. Thus, in our politically mediatized times, the former *common ground* provided by shared mass media news has not only been politically and discursively reshaped, but also fragmented into multiple realities, platforms and voices, depending on the audiences' habits and cultures of mediatization (Block, 2013; Hepp, 2013).

In a way, today's political communication environment is not anymore about humans using communication to inform or be politically informed about politics, or to develop political dialogues, but about platforms and algorithms organizing political and public life for us, a claim that has become palpable, first through the Cambridge Analytica Trump election scandal (Cadwalladr & Graham-Harrison, 2018); and four years later through the Twitter banning of accounts from extremist organizations and personalities during the US 2020 elections, notably Trump's account (see "Twitter 'permanently suspends'", 2021), or Google and Facebook's blocking the circulation of news media content among its subscribers in Australia (see "Google says", 2021). The world has been witnessing how media platforms have become key gatekeepers of political news with a power of moderation that sways depending on political and profit-driven circumstances. Media platforms have been more transparent than ever before about the fact that they are not a public service, but private businesses driven by profit and/or their own partisan interest. The owners of media platforms (and their designated 'moderators'), have become sophisticated substitutes of 19th and 20th centuries press barons.

Ultimately, as Palacio Martin (2017) indicated, what makes populist players more dangerous is that, in their quest for power, they use the media to mobilize the language and ideas that once belonged to pluralist democracy but precisely "to undermine its pluralist nature" (para. 2).

3.3 Discursive disruption

I have now reached my third theoretical theme that involves the construction of the concept of discursive disruption itself, a conceptual and analytical framework that serves to identify, analyze, and understand disruptions in the discourses and conventions of modern democracy. The study of democratic disruptions is not new as scholarly discussions about how democracy has declined abound, especially today, after the controversial and discordant Trump presidency in the US.

Norris and Inglehart (2019) and Inglehart and Norris (2016), explored the connection between populism and democracy for years. They sought explanations about why "Rising support for populist parties has disrupted the politics of many Western societies" as well as "long established patterns of party competition" (Inglehart & Norris, 2016, p. 1). Their work is based on a comparative analysis of surveys, patterns of party competition, and the examination of two theories that underpin their views of populism, culture, and democratic democracy. First, Inglehart and Norris (2016) proposed the "economic insecurity perspective", which focuses on the reactions of the workforce and society "to changes in post-industrial economies" (p. 1); second, they proposed the "cultural backlash thesis", which suggests that the rise of populism is the reaction of formerly predominant cultural groups to dramatic changes in values and traditional ways of life in societies that are now more liberal, open, and prone to advocate for civil rights. Inglehart and Norris (2016) concluded that, "Western societies face more unpredictable contests, antiestablishment populist challenges to the legitimacy of liberal democracy, and potential disruptions to long-established patterns of party competition" (p. 31). Their research raises important questions, especially about the role of culture and populism in democratic dysfunctions.

A different kind of reflection was developed by Post-Marxist discourse philosopher Ernesto Laclau (2005). In Spanish the word disruption does not exist, and is generally translated as interruption or rupture. In an article about Hugo Chávez's populist leadership, Laclau (2005) described the populist rupture, or *"la ruptura populista"*, as a momentous event that occurs when a "dichotomization of the social space has taken place, and actors see themselves as participants in one or the other of the opposing fields" (p. 56). Laclau suggested populism as a breakage of the polity where the identity (image or impression) of *"los de abajo"* (the oppressed, the dispossessed) is constructed in terms of a "collective actor" (the people), destined to take power from the unpopular ruling elites, a process facilitated through culture, namely, shared symbols and "the emergence of a leader" (p. 56) as the "agglutinating factor" (p. 60) in the construction of the people.

Laclau's (2005) emphasis on how populist players employ *the people* as a political construct and "empty signifier" led me to explore a different albeit related kind of disruption: Identity disruption. Preece (2016) argued that "those who feel that they belong have no need to worry about their identities. Identity only becomes an issue when a person's sense of belonging is disrupted" (p. 2). Preece (2016) described identity disruption in terms of an "'out of place' feeling that gives rise to identity work and creates opportunities for new subjectivities through the interaction of the 'old' and the 'new'" (p. 2). Identity disruption involves two dimensions, one positive, inclusive and innovative, which identifies an enriched existence resulting from a merging of identities that may result in increased recognition and improved ways of life; and one negative and exclusive, which may lead to intolerance and ruptures in society.

Moreover, the use of online media spaces is an expression of a different type of disruption, called by Schmidt and Cohen (2010) "digital disruption". These writers argued that digital disruption would involve more collaborative work between traditional and digital news organizations and actors (citizens, journalists). However, Schmidt and Cohen (2010) also suggested that when applied to politics, digital disruption would mean that the most powerful states would face "huge challenges to established ways of governing" (p. 75), where communication technologies would "carve out spaces for democracy as well as autocracy and empower individuals for both good and ill" (p. 75).

Developments in countries that have been governed by populist leaders (such as the cases of the US and Venezuela), suggest that some of the main indicators of democracy—pluralism, rule of law, electoral integrity, separation of powers, tolerance, accountability, and the promotion of freedoms and rights—have been challenged by the antagonistic discourse of such leaders. Populist players have not only tapped into the antipolitical frustrations of their constituents and exposed the failures of the traditional political elite, but also have challenged the constitutions of their countries, which Hobbes (2015, p. 24) called "the pacts and covenants by which the parts of this body politic were first made, set together, and united".

In sum, the discursive disruption frame that I propose here views populism as communicative violence, as a *rupture*, a cultural reaction to plural debate, liberal ideas, and civil rights. *A communicative kind of violence that disrupts, undermines, or shatters democracy from within, blocking or closing plural political dialogue in the process.*

Hence, respect, acceptance, or dismissal vis-à-vis the indicators traditionally associated with conventional Western democracy is one of the variables considered in my analysis of Chávez's and Trump's communicative styles.

I also have proposed discursive disruption as the opposite concepts of Dryzek's (2002) discursive democracy, and Young's (1997a) communicative democracy. Discursive disruption is a framework that helps analyze how the language, rules of interaction and conventions of modern democracy, that is, the flow of democratic communication, are transgressed or interrupted through populist speech performances that are not only critical but antagonistic vis-à-vis plural democracy.

The discursive disruption process or logic evokes what Adorno (1973) called "totality", as it is embedded in the same principles proposing that, "By removing contradiction by contradiction...we also remove dialectics" (p. 161). When "facts and fairness" are transgressed through words or speech acts, the danger is that powerful populist leaders like Chávez and Trump get away with "subverting the system" (Rohde, 2019, para. 12).

References

A letter on justice and open debate. (2020, July 7). *Harper's Magazine*. https://harpers.org/a-letter-on-justice-and-open-debate/

Aalberg, T., Esser, F., Reinemann, C., Strömbäck, J., & de Vreese, C. H. (2017). *Populist political communication in Europe*. Routledge.

Adorno, T. W. (1973). *Negative dialectics*. Seabury Press.

Almond, G., & Verba, S. (1965). *Civic culture*. Little, Brown.

Arendt, H. (1998). *The human condition*. The University of Chicago Press.

Banks, J. (2010). Regulating hate speech online. *International Review of Law, Computers & Technology, 24*(3), 233–239.

Blair, K. L. (2017). Did secretary Clinton lose to a 'basket of deplorables'? An examination of islamophobia, homophobia, sexism and conservative ideology in the 2016 US presidential election. *Psychology & Sexuality, 8*(4), 334–355. https://doi.org/10.1080/19419899.2017.1397051

Block, E. (2013). A culturalist approach to the concept of the mediatization of politics: The age of "media hegemony". *Communication Theory, 23*(3), 259–278. https://doi.org/10.1111/comt.12016

Block, E. (2015). *Political communication and leadership. Mimetization, Hugo Chávez and the construction of power and identity*. Routledge.

Block, E., & Negrine, R. (2017). The populist communication style: Toward a critical framework. *International Journal of Communication, 11*, 20.

Bolivar, A. (2018). *Political discourse as dialogue. A Latin American perspective*. Routledge.

Bouvier, G. (2020). Racist call-outs and cancel culture on Twitter: The limitations of the platform's ability to define issues of social justice. *Discourse, Context & Media, 38,* 100431.

Bracciale, R., & Martella, A. (2017). Define the populist political communication style: The case of Italian political leaders on Twitter. *Information, Communication & Society, 20*(9), 1310–1329.

Caballero, M. (2010). *Historia de los venezolanos del siglo XX.* Editorial Alfa.

Cadwalladr, C., & Graham-Harrison, E. (2018, March 18). Revealed: 50 million Facebook profiles harvested for Cambridge Analytica in major data breach. *The Guardian.* https://www.theguardian.com/news/2018/mar/17/cambridge-analytica-facebook-influence-us-election

Canovan, M. (1999). Trust the people! Populism and the two faces of democracy. *Political Studies, 47*(1), 2–16.

Castro-Leiva, L. (1999). *Sed buenos ciudadanos.* Alfadil Ediciones, Alfa Grupo Editorial.

Constitucion de la Republica Bolivariana de Venezuela. (1999). Tribunal supremo de Justicia. *Gaceta Oficial Extraordinaria* N° 5. 453. http://www.tsj.gov.ve/legislacion/constitucion1999.htm

de Tocqueville, A. (2003). *Democracy in America* (B. Frohnen, Ed.), *10.* Regnery. (Original work published 1835).

Dryzek, J. (2002). *Deliberative democracy and beyond: Liberals, critics, contestations.* Oxford University Press. https://www.oxfordscholarship.com/view/10.1093/019925043X.001.0001/acprof-9780199250431

Ernst, N., Blassnig, S., Engesser, S., Büchel, F., & Esser, F. (2019). Populists prefer social media over talk shows: An analysis of populist messages and stylistic elements across six countries. *Social Media + Society, 5*(1). https://doi.org/10.1177/2056305118823358

Escalante-Block, E. (2018). Hugo Chávez's use of emotional appeals. *Comunicazione politica, 19*(1), 51–72.

Fake news & post truth: How world changed in 2016. (2016, December 21). *BBC News.* [Video]. https://www.youtube.com/watch?v=8QVqwNLJb7s

Farrelly, M. (2015). *Discourse and democracy: Critical analysis of the language of government.* Routledge. https://www.amazon.com/Discourse-Democracy-Critical-Government-Routledge-ebook/dp/B00O1PQRLQ

Foucault, M. (1972). *The archeology of knowledge and the discourse on language.* Pantheon.

Gelbei, K. (2011). *Speech matters: Getting free speech right* (1st ed.). University of Queensland Press.

Google says it will remove search function in Australia if media code becomes law (2021, January 21). *CNBC.* https://www.cnbc.com/2021/01/22/google-says-it-will-remove-search-function-in-australia-if-media-code-becomes-law.html

Habermas, J. (1984). *The theory of communicative action: Vol. 1 reason and the rationalization of society.* Beacon Press.

Hameleers, M. (2019). The populism of online communities: Constructing the boundary between "blameless" people and "culpable" others. *Communication Culture & Critique, 12*(1), 147–165.

Hanson, R. L. (1989). Democracy. In T. Ball, J. Farr, & R. L. Hanson (Eds.), *Political innovation and conceptual change* (pp. 68–89). Cambridge University Press.

Hawkins, K. (2010). *Venezuela's chavismo and populism in comparative perspective*. Cambridge University Press.

Hepp, A. (2013). *Cultures of mediatization*. John Wiley & Sons.

Hobbes, T. (2015). *Leviathan*. Chios Classics.

Howard, J. W. (2020). Free speech and hate speech. *Annual Review of Political Science, 22*, 93–109. https://www.annualreviews.org/doi/pdf/10.1146/annurev-polisci-051517-012343

Inglehart, R. F., & Norris, P. (2016, August). Trump, Brexit, and the rise of populism: Economic have-nots and cultural backlash (HKS Working Paper No. RWP16-026). *SSRN*. http://dx.doi.org/10.2139/ssrn.2818659

Israel, J. (2009). *A revolution of the mind: Radical enlightenment and the intellectual origins of modern democracy*. Princeton University Press. https://www.amazon.com/Revolution-Mind-Enlightenment-Intellectual-Democracy/dp/0691152608

Jagers, J., & Walgrave, S. (2007). Populism as political communication style: An empirical study of political parties' discourse in Belgium. *European Journal of Political Research, 46*, 319–345.

Kayam, O. (2018). Donald Trump's rhetoric. *Language and Dialogue, 8*(2), 183–208.

Kitzberger, P. (2020, June, n.d.). Polarización, Prensa y libertad de expresión en Venezuela. *Nueva Sociedad*. https://nuso.org/articulo/polarizacion-prensa-y-libertad-de-expresion-en-venezuela/

Krämer, B. (2014). Media populism: A conceptual clarification and some theses on its effects. *Communication Theory, 24*(1), 42–60. https://doi-org.ezproxy.library.uq.edu.au/10.1111/comt.12029

Kriesi, H. (2013). Introduction—The new challenges to democracy. In *Democracy in the age of globalization and mediatization* (pp. 1–16). Palgrave Macmillan.

Kriesi, H. (2018). Revisiting the populist challenge. *Politologický časopis-Czech Journal of Political Science, 25*(1), 5–27.

Laclau, E. (2005). La deriva populista y la centroizquierda Latinoamericana [the populist drift and the Latin American centre-right]. *Nueva Sociedad, 89*, 56–61.

Levitsky, S., & Loxton, J. (2013). Populism and competitive authoritarianism in the Andes. *Democratization, 20(*1), 107–136. https://doi.org/10.1080/135103 47.2013.738864

Lewis, P., Barr, C., Clarke, S., Voce, A., Levett, C., & Gutiérrez, P. (2019, March 7). Revealed: The rise and rise of populist rhetoric. *The Guardian*. https://www.theguardian.com/world/ng-interactive/2019/mar/06/revealed-the-rise-and-rise-of-populist-rhetoric

Mazzoleni, G. (2003). The media and the growth of neo-populism in contemporary democracies. In G. Mazzoleni, J. Stewart, & B. Horsfield (Eds.), *The media and neo-populism: A contemporary comparative analysis* (pp. 1–20). Praeger.

Mazzoleni, G., & Bracciale, R. (2018). Socially mediated populism: The communicative strategies of political leaders on Facebook. *Palgrave Communications, 4*(1), 50.

Moffitt, B., & Tormey, S. (2014). Rethinking populism: Politics, mediatisation and political style. *Political Studies, 62*(2), 381–397.

Mudde, C., & Rovira Kaltwasser, C. (2018). Studying populism in comparative perspective: Reflections on the contemporary and future research agenda. *Comparative Political Studies, 51*(13), 1667–1693.

Norris, P. (2016, March 11). It is not Trump. Authoritarian populism in rising across the West. Here is how. *The Washington Post.* https://www.washingtonpost.com/news/monkey-cage/wp/2016/03/11/its-not-just-trump-authoritarian-populism-is-rising-across-the-west-heres-why/

Norris, P. (2020). *Closed minds? Is a 'cancel culture' stifling academic freedom and intellectual debate in political science?* (HKS Working Paper No. RWP20-025). Harvard.

Norris, P., & Inglehart, R. (2019). *Cultural backlash: The rise of authoritarian-populism.* Cambridge University Press.

O'Neill, J. (2002). The rhetoric of deliberation: Some problems in Kantian theories of deliberative democracy. *Res Publica, 8,* 249–268.

Palacio Martin, J. (2017, October 23). El tiempo de la confusion democratica. *El Pais.* https://elpais.com/elpais/2017/10/20/opinion/1508513890_107029.html

Papacharissi, Z. (2021). *After democracy: Imagining our political future.* Yale University Press.

Pateman, C. (1970). *Participation and democratic theory.* Cambridge University Press.

Pew Research Centre. (2017, October 16). *Globally, broad support for representative and direct democracy. But many also endorse nondemocratic alternatives.* http://www.pewglobal.org/2017/10/16/globally-broad-support-for-representative-and-direct-democracy/

Pino-Iturrieta, E. (2006). El Mito del hombre fuerte y bueno. Ideas para un estudio que pueda matar a gomez. In G. Carrera Damas, C. Leal-Curiel, G. Lomne, & F. Martinez (Eds.), *Mitos politicos en la siciedades andinas. Origenes, invenciones y ficciones* (pp. 269–278). Editorial Equinoccio (Universidad Simon Bolivar).

Postill, J. (2018). Populism and social media: A global perspective. *Media, Culture & Society, 40*(5), 754–765. https://doi.org/10.1177/0163443718772186.

Preece, S. (2016). *Introduction: Language and identity in applied linguistics.* Routledge.

Rhodan, M. (2017, April 24). Read Barack Obama's first public remarks since leaving office. *Time.* https://time.com/4753027/barack-obama-university-of-chicago-speech-transcript/

Rohde, D. (2019, December 9). In Congress and at the Justice Department, a bad day for facts, fairness, and the future. *The New Yorker.* https://www.newyorker.com/news/daily-comment/in-congress-and-at-the-justice-department-a-bad-day-for-fact-fairness-and-the-future

Schmidt, E., & Cohen, J. (2010). The digital disruption: Connectivity and the diffusion of power. *Foreign Affairs, 89*(6), 75–85. https://www.researchgate. net/publication/259854536_The_Digital_Disruption_Connectivity_and_the_ Diffusion_of_Power

Silverstein, M. (2003). *Talking politics: The substance of style from Abe to "W".* Prickly Paradigm Press.

Sonenscher, M. (Ed). (2003). *Sieyès: Political writings: Including the debate between Sieyes and Tom Paine in 1791.* Hackett Publishing.

Steinmetz, K. (2017, June 19). Portland's mayor on protests, riots and the 'missing middle'. *Time.* https://time.com/4824299/portland-protests-ted-wheeler-alt-right-antifa/

Swart, J., Peters, C., & Broersma, M. (2019). Sharing and discussing news in private social media groups: The social function of news and current affairs in location-based, work-oriented and leisure-focused communities. *Digital Journalism, 7*(2), 187–205. https://doi.org/10.1080/21670811.2018.1465351

Tharoor, I. (2017 January 26). Trump is the U.S.'s first Latin American president. *The Washington Post.* https://www.washingtonpost.com/news/worldviews/ wp/2017/01/26/trump-is-the-u-s-s-first-latin-american-president/

Trump impeachment trial: Biden warns democracy is fragile. (2021, February 21). *BBC.* https://www.bbc.com/news/world-us-canada-56061100

Twitter 'permanently suspends' Trump's account. (2021, January 9). *BBC.* https://www.bbc.com/news/world-us-canada-55597840

Vaccari, C., & Valeriani, A. (2018). *Digital political talk and political participation: Comparing established and third wave democracies.* Sage Open. https:// doi.org/10.1177/2158244018784986

Viroli, M. (1993). Machiavelli and the republican idea of politics. In G. Bock, Q. Skinner, & M. Viroli (Eds.), *Machiavelli and republicanism, 18* (pp. 143–171). Cambridge University Press.

Von Vacano, D. (2019). American caudillo: Princely performative populism and democracy in the Americas. *Philosophy & Social Criticism, 45*(4), 413–428. https://doi.org/10.1177/0191453719826349

Waisbord, S. (2003). Media populism: Neo-populism in Latin America. In G. Mazzoleni, J. Stewart, & B. Horsfield (Eds.), *The media and neo-populism, to contemporary comparative analysis* (pp. 198–216). Praeger.

Welsch, F. F., Carrasquero, J. V., & Varnagy, D. (2004). Cultura politica, democracia y capital social en Venezuela: Perspectiva comparada. In Programa de las Naciones Unidas para el Desarrollo–PNUD (2004). *Valores y cultura politica de los Venezolanos: Hablan los investigadores* (pp. 59–77). PNUD.

Williams, R. (1977). *Marxism and literature.* Oxford University Press.

Worsley, P. (1969). The concept of populism. In G. Ionescu, & E. Gellner (Eds.), *Populism: Its meaning and national characteristics* (pp. 212–250). Macmillan.

Yasseri, T., Hale, S., John, P., & Margetts, H. (2016). *Political turbulence: How social media shape collective action.* Princeton University Press.

Young, I. M. (1997a). *Intersecting voices: Dilemmas of gender, political philosophy, and policy*. Princeton University Press.

Young, I. M. (1997b). Difference as a resource for democratic communication. In J. Bohman & W. Rehg (Eds.), *Deliberative democracy: Essays on reason and politics* (pp. 383–404). MIT Press. https://ebookcentral-proquest-com. ezproxy.library.uq.edu.au/lib/uql/detail.action?docID=3338820#

Young, I. M. (2000). *Inclusion and democracy*. Oxford University Press.

4 The discursive disruption framework

As I have shown in the previous three chapters, democratic erosion saw a significant increase during the first two decades of the 21st century when, coincidentally or not, populist leaders rose to power and their rhetoric became pervasive. My aim is to identify some patterns and links between those events. To undertake this task, I have advanced a conceptual and analytical framework—discursive disruption—that can help to recognize, analyze, and understand populist speech performances with the power to undermine democratic discourses and conventions in specific groups or societies, using Chávez's Venezuela and Trump's US as case studies and illustrations. In Chapter 3, I developed the *conceptual* dimension of the framework that resulted from the interconnection of three theoretical themes: (a) authoritarian populist communication; (b) democratic discourses; and (c) the concept of discursive disruption as such. Now, in Chapter 4, I build the *analytical* dimension of the framework consisting of a set of variables whereby I analyze speech performances by two prominent populist presidents, Hugo Chávez and Donald Trump, my case studies.

The set of variables displayed in this chapter will serve to analyze specific texts that include Chávez's and Trump's speeches, statements, policy as well as selected pieces of news media coverage of those performances (as metadiscourse); I explore whether and how these items together reveal disruptions in their respective polities. As Deacon et al. (2021) suggested, media in all its forms should be investigated by communication scholars, as "Legacy media, social media and their various hybrids play a major role in organizing the routines and rituals or everyday life" (p. 2). The unity of language and social life was also at the heart of Dell Hymes's (1967) view of communication, as he argued that "Facets of the cultural values and beliefs, social institutions and forms, roles and personalities, history and ecology of a community must be examined together in relation to communicative events and

DOI: 10.4324/9781003118602-4

patterns as focus of study" (p. 3). Following Hymes's (1967) advice, the analysis I undertake in this book intends to reflect some of the ways language, communication, politics, and society are intertwined.

The present chapter explains and supports the mixed qualitative method I use in this investigation, which consists of two case studies and textual analysis executed through an updated and adjusted version of Hymes's (1972) ethnography of communication. I study Chávez's and Trump's speeches, policy, and their news media coverage during specific periods of their campaigns and governments. I analyze these texts vis-à-vis an expanded version of the discursive disruption variables that were drawn from the conceptual framework in Chapter 3: Language, identity, and use of the media, to which I now add the acceptance or dismissal of democratic discourses, values, and conventions.

However, first I must start by explaining and justifying the selection of my two case studies. To do it, I will present the findings of a pilot study that I conducted as a preresearch or background study. The results of this study supported the decision of studying Chávez and Trump as paradigms of populist communication.

It is important to clarify that the pilot study *should not be confused with the main method* used in this book. This preliminary and rather informal piece of research both paved the way and contributed to the approach that I finally took to build the analytical framework that I present in the second and third sections of this chapter and apply in Chapter 5 to study the two cases.

4.1 Pilot study: The Chávez-Trump déjà vu

The pilot study ran three informal digital searches in the global news media, using the keywords Chávez, Trump, differences, similarities. The first search was in 2016/2017, when I started to become interested in the topic, and later, in 2019, when I set in motion the research for this book. The sample comprised 78 news articles or texts ($N = 78$) of which 82.05% were articles that supported the comparison and mentioned strong similarities between Trump and Chávez, while 17.94% of the texts highlighted the differences between Chávez and Trump.

Due to its newsworthiness, this topic—the Chávez-Trump similarities and differences—got the attention of the global news media. A body of international correspondents, Latin American commentators, and Venezuelan journalists suggested having "déjà vu" feelings when they listened to Trump. I ran an informal Google search that covered the period 2015–2019, using the keywords: Similarities Differences

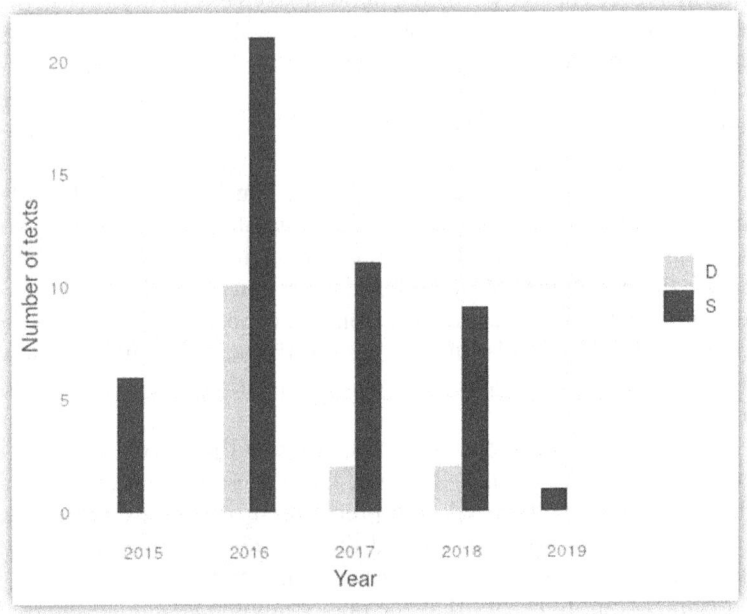

Figure 4.1 Similarities (S) and Differences (D) Chávez-Trump 2015–2019

Hugo Chávez Donald Trump, which after collection, cleaning, and coding rendered 63 texts that I stored digitally and analyzed manually. The results, 80.95% of the sample (*n* = 51 texts), produced articles that supported the comparison and mentioned similarities between Trump and Chávez. Figure 4.1 shows how the news media comparisons between Chávez and Trump increased in 2016, the year of the presidential elections in the US.

Conversely, 19.04% of the sample (*n* = 12 texts) stressed Chávez's and Trump's differences, among which were ideological and cultural differences, opposite social and cultural backgrounds, the ineffectiveness of the comparison, and the differences between inclusionary and exclusionary populism. For other commentators, the comparison that Chávez-Trump embodied was a "cultural generalization", which some found offensive toward Chávez and Venezuela.

Figure 4.2 shows a heatmap of the main topics of difference and similarity, plotted using the software R language for statistical analysis (R Foundation, 2018). Topics coded as 1, 2, 3, A, B, and R were the most salient. These corresponded, respectively, to: (1) appeal to the people; (2) use of insulting language; (3) use of/controversial relations

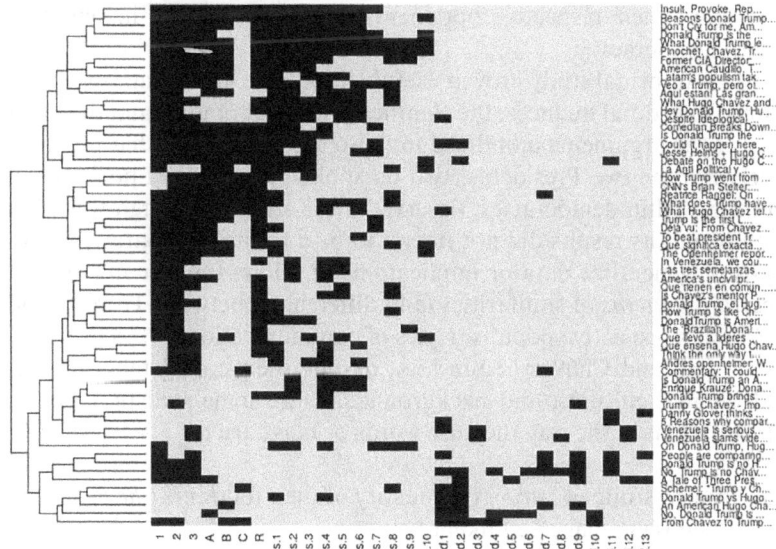

Figure 4.2 Heatmap: Topics of Similarities and Differences Between Chávez-Trump 2015–2019

with news media; (A) authoritarian, narcissistic tone; (B) polarizing positions; (C) bypassing law and institutions; (R) triggers ruptures, unrest, disruptions.

Rory Carroll (2013), a British correspondent who covered Chávez for years, and who has also covered Trump, was one of the first journalists to draw attention to the similarities between the two leaders arguing that "Language is key, notably humor, insults and vulgarity to rupture protocol and connect with supporters on a gut level" (para. 13).

The inclusionary and exclusionary character of the different types of populism was raised by Tim Gill (2016) in his article rejecting the comparison between Chávez and Trump; Gill argued that Chávez empowered the marginalized and included millions of previously excluded Venezuelans in the social, political, and economic life of the country, through his discourse and also his social policy. Trump, instead, he argued had excluded non-Americans in his discourse and also in his first policy proposal (his travel bans) and sought to exclude many Americans on the basis of religion or race. However, Corrales (cited in Smilde, 2016) refuted Gill's thesis by arguing that both Chávez and Trump shared the use of exclusionary and intolerant discourses to confront their respective opponents, a practice that is inconsistent with democracy.

This informal study proved useful; despite the dissenting voices and some anecdotal nuances, the significant number of texts and the quality of the arguments mobilized in these texts suggested that the links between the two Presidents, two outspoken populists in positions of power within democracies, deserved more study. Although this pilot study and its results did not intend to be a formal comparative analysis or generalize data or implications, it allows the visualization of certain *patterns* of similarities (and differences) between Trump's and Chávez's respective populist styles of communication.

Trump and Chávez before him, despite their completely different ideologies, cultures, and backgrounds, share some stylistic traits or inclinations in the way they use words or language to:

a   Successfully *construct* the identity of their followers (*the people*) in their own image and likeness.
b   *Communicate* their politics and governance in divisive, aggressive, and antagonistic ways.
c   Rise to power as *antipolitical outsiders, critical of democracy but within democracy*.
d   Use the media effectively to confront mainstream journalists and news media outlets.
e   Trigger disturbances in their respective polities. For example, unrest and demonstrations increased in Chávez's and Trump's respective countries almost immediately after their election, and there were transgressions of traditional diplomatic or political language and protocols, as I am going to show in Chapter 5.

The informal results rendered by the pilot study showed certain trends that deserved closer and critical exploration. This explains why I expanded my investigation of Chávez's and Trump's communication styles, searching for: (a) communicative and discursive patterns, that is, similarities, differences, and links between the two; and (b) the impact of their communicative styles and strategies on disruptions and erosions in their countries' democratic discourses.

4.2 Approach to the analysis and method

As Dell Hymes (1972) suggested, the study of specific styles of communication, especially when they are typical of particular groups, entails shaping a vocabulary, a speech "taxonomy" or framework through which we can gain a systematic understanding of speech events with the power to disrupt the discourses of democracy. The discursive disruption analytical framework proposed by this book, on the one side, facilitates the acquisition of knowledge through the analysis of populist speech performances and communicative strategies that have upset or unsettled democratic discourses in some countries; and, on the other, offers an analytical tool to critically evaluate and interrogate such cases. The concept of discursive disruption is a small contribution toward a very much needed update of the vocabularies of democracy and political communication, which, I propose, should incorporate the characteristics and implications of the disruptive populist talk.

More broadly, discursive disruption helps assess the communicative and discursive character of the mediation between "politics" and "the political". Martin (2013) defined "politics" as the routines, conventions, and norms of interaction administering the polity, and "the political" as the abstract frames, principles, and ideologies that define that polity; thus "the political names a dimension of controversy and potentially violence". (p. 4). The political is the dimension that marks the identity, "being" or ethos of the polity. Taken together, politics and the political embody a set of discourses, which in the specific case of this book, refers to discourses of modern democracy that have been disrupted or eroded in the last two decades. Those surveys pointed to an increase of polarization and division, which in turn have led to democracy's legitimacy loss in the case studies evaluated by this book. I am particularly interested in "the political", that is, whether and how certain disruptive or conflictive discourses reshaped the ethos or character of the polities in my two case studies.

So, in this way, the discursive disruption framework can also help to visualize more effectively the legitimating and normalizing power of words (Van Leeuwen, 2007), a power that is executed, among other categories, "through narratives whose outcomes reward legitimate actions and punish non-legitimate actions." (p. 91). Narratives which, I suggest, embody the bad logic and faulty reasoning that rhetoric associates with "logical fallacies" (Heinrich, 2007). Populist leaders, as I illustrate in Chapter 5, employ fallacious appeals to connect and bond with their audiences through emotions and irrationality, rather than reason, arguments, or logic, by using, for example, fear appeals suggesting that actions that go against what the speaker says will have consequences that involve some sort of punishment. Fear appeals compel people to act in certain ways, and such compulsion, as Heinrich (2007) suggested "precludes choice". Populist leaders also employ appeals to authority and closure, as, no matter how questionable or irrational, what the speaker says should always be accepted without deliberation, which also suggests a tendency to intolerance and requests for absolute loyalty. And populist leaders frequently use the ad hominem fallacy that, as I mentioned previously, is a direct, humiliating, abusive attack on specific opponents' dignity (Heinrich, 2007).

The fear, authority, and ad hominem appeals tend to change attitudes and behavior by "creating anxiety in those receiving the fearful message" (Simpson, 2017, p. 1). Strategic communication scholars have argued that these types of basic or "drive" appeals, are effective communicative tactics based on negative emotions that "motivate instrumental responding" (Meczkowski & Dillard, 2017, p. 1) through a mixture of "fear and persuasion" (p. 2). As I noted in an earlier chapter, populists, such as Chávez and Trump, have strategically used emotional appeals to connect with their constituents and obtain endorsement for their policies (Escalante-Block, 2018). These types of appeals often lead to what Sartori (2002) called the "emotionalization of politics" (p.119), which describes a process that reduces politics to emotional episodes mainly by using the media, which today would have to consider 'the media' in all its forms, especially the use of media platforms that dominate our everyday life. Sartori (2002) argued that emotional mediatic episodes consist of "red-hot messages that stir our emotions, ignite our feelings, excite our senses and, ultimately, make us passionate" (p. 119). Populist players are skillful operators of culture, language, emotions, identity, and media in ways that resonate with a significant group of their constituents' political frustrations and disenchantment, which in turn creates bonds and develops strong ties of trust and loyalty over time.

4.3 The discursive disruption analytical framework

This section proceeds to expand on the qualitative mixed method that I use in my analysis: (a) two case studies consisting of Venezuela's Hugo Chávez's and the US's Donald Trump's speech performances produced during their first and last presidential campaigns, and their first period in office; (b) textual analysis of those speech performances that include speeches, statements, policy, and their respective media coverage; and (c) critical analysis of disruptive events that have been considered to have emerged from, or were triggered by Chávez's and Trump's talk.

Thomas (2011) argued that case studies are "analyses of persons, events, decisions, periods, projects, policies, institutions, or other systems that are studied holistically by one or more methods" (p. 513). Case studies constitute one of the main methods whereby research is undertaken in communication, politics, and the social sciences in general. However, despite, or perhaps because of their popularity, case studies need a clear structure, that is, a framework or typology. Thus, case studies should develop analytical frameworks or *typologies* that fulfill a double function, as the study is conducted within that frame, and such frame also serves to illustrate, explain, and support the phenomenon studied. This means that a case study comprises two elements: (a) a "subject" or "practical, historical unity" (Thomas, 2011, p. 513) represented here by Chávez's and Trump's communicative styles; and (b) a theoretical frame, or "object" of the study, embodied in the theoretical and analytical frames developed in Chapters 3 and 4. Thomas (2011) also argued that developing a frame or typology helps to test the variables considered in the design of the case study. This book's proposed set of variables are tested in Chapter 5.

I analyze my two case studies through two levels of variables drawn from the theoretical discussion developed in Chapter 3. On the first, broader level, the texts are analyzed through the variables in the populist communication framework proposed by Block and Negrine (2017) that involves the analysis of the way populists use or construct (1) their speech or language (often antagonistic, abrasive, using emotional, ad hominem, fear or authority appeals), (2) identity (manipulation of patriotism, nationalism, cultural symbols, class, religion, and race), and (3) news media (populist actors' own use of all forms of media, as well as their relationship with journalists and/or news media outlets). On the second level, from the discussions on democracy in Chapter 3 surged a fourth variable, not included by Block and Negrine (2017) in their frame, or by other scholars of populism, at least not in the same way I employ it here. This variable, which is crucial to my inquiry, consists of Chávez's and Trump's acceptance or dismissal of the main variables or indicators that have been traditionally associated with discourses of modern democracy. For analytical purposes, this fourth variable was broken down into three sub-variables, namely, (a) respect for democratic freedoms, civil rights, and social justice, (b) respect for separation of power and rule of law, and (c) respect for plural and rational political dialogue and free and fair elections. See the graphic version of the discursive disruption analytical framework in Figure 4.3.

Case studies (Populist leaders in positions of power)		Chávez (Speech performances)	Trump (Speech performances)
Discursive Disruption Variables	Language		
	Identity/Culture		
	Relationship with media		
	Acceptance or dismissal of democratic values and conventions		
	(a) Respect for democratic freedoms, civil rights, and social justice		
	(b) Respect for separation of powers and rule of law		
	(c) Respect for plural and rational dialogue and free and fair elections		

Figure 4.3 Discursive Disruption Analytical Framework: Key Variables

The variables shown above drove the collection, selection, and analysis of the texts in the sample, be they leaders' speeches or statements, proposed policy, or news media coverage (I expand on the sampling method a few paragraphs below).

I analyze the texts (speeches, statements, policy, news media coverage) in Chávez's and Trump's cases as they are represented, or occur, in different communicative venues, by using a loose and unstructured version of Hymes's (1967; 1972) ethnography of communication "social units" of analysis, namely: (a) "speech situations", a term that describes ceremonial situations, such as presidential inaugurations, the opening of parliament, UN addresses, etc.; (b) "speech events" occur within speech situations, for example, the protocols that guide and moderate presidential or parliamentary debates, TV shows, or social platform protocols; and, (c) "speech acts", which are the individual utterances that form the minimal, and probably the most salient unit of analysis, such as, pronouncements, announcements, insults, demands, jokes, emotional appeals of different kinds (e.g., fear appeals), policy propositions, or tweets. I often use the term *speech performance* in the discussion to represent a mix of the above.

Also, I use an adjusted and updated version of Hymes's (1972) "components" of speech, which are the most minute, specific units through which I will analyze Chávez's and Trump's texts, as well as texts corresponding to their coverage in the news media. I analyze the texts in terms of some of the following components (when they are relevant and in no specific order): context, speaker, goals, message, tone, language, style, norms, genre or format, and channel or platform of communication.

The analyses of news media texts corresponding to *media coverage or analysis* of Chávez's and Trump's respective speech performances, as well as signs of democratic disruptions triggered by such performances, are fundamental to the analysis in Chapter 5 and discussion in Chapter 6. Sclafani (2018) suggested that political speech is not only defined by common language but also by common linguistic forms, cultural contexts, social norms, and the "increased number of channels of political media discourse" (p. 8). Media discourses provide the mediatized context, or environment, that surrounds political speech, which Sclafani (2018) called "metadiscourse". Metadiscourse can take multiple forms—news reports, articles, editorials, interviews, talk shows, tweets, retweets, or comments on tweets or other social media channels and platforms—surrounding the activities and remarks of politicians disseminated through all forms of news media. This explains why I incorporate news coverage and editorials about Chávez's and Trump's speech performances and government as key contextual *metadiscursive* elements. These metadiscursive elements will help me not only to assess how Chávez's and Trump's discursive actions and decisions are represented by the news media but also, and more importantly, if those speeches have led to disruptions in their respective polities.

As suggested earlier, this study is a mix of theoretical inquiry and illustrative study, less concerned with generating "extensive perspectives" leading to generalization, than with providing "intensive insights into complex human and social phenomena" (Deacon et al., 2021, p. 108). I use elements from the theoretical architecture laid-out in Chapter 3, to develop the variables through which I will analyze the two case studies' (Chávez and Trump) selected speech performances or texts. The selected texts to be analyzed consist of nonrandom purposively selected "typical" and "critical" sample units. Thus the mixed sampling technique includes "typical-case sampling" (Deacon et al., 2021, p. 122), which allows me to identify texts that exemplify "the key features of the phenomenon being investigated" (p. 122), and "critical-case sampling" which facilitates the selection of texts that exhibit "the credible, dramatic properties of the 'test case'" (p. 123). Using this mixed sampling technique assists me not only to test Chávez's and Trump's speech performances against the variables but also to identify disruptions or transgressions in democratic discourses that originated in communicative events or acts.

The selected texts that I use to illustrate and support the discursive disruption framework, (mainly public speeches, statements, and their coverage) were collected from digital official (governmental) archives and libraries, major search engines (mainly Google and Factiva), news media outlets' archives, and web and social media relevant platforms.

The news media texts were collected from the most followed global and national (US, Venezuela) digital legacy news media outlets (e.g., *CNN, ABC, BBC, Reuters, AP, The Guardian, The New York Times, Washington Post, Huffington Post, Al Jazeera, Telesur, RT, El Nacional, El Universal, Ultimas Noticias, La Patilla, Efecto Cocuyo*, among others). I also selected some typical social media material, mainly from Trump's and Chávez's Twitter posts, which are considered as speech acts.

Due to the differences in Chávez's and Trump's times in office, the periods of analysis differ. I analyze (a) texts published during their campaign years (Chávez's four presidential campaigns in 1988, 2000, 2006, and 2012, and Trump's two campaigns in 2016 and 2020), and (b) texts published during their first 4 years in office (Chávez 1999–2005 during his first extended period, where he was elected twice, the second in 2000 under the new constitution; and 2007–2011 in his second period; and Trump's four years in office from 2017 to 2020). One of the reasons that explains this decision is the way Trump and Chávez have used the media of the time; Chávez used TV and print media to communicate in 1998; however, Twitter became his favorite channel of direct communication with his constituents during his last campaign in 2012 until he died in 2013. Trump's 2016 campaign was characterized by his intense use of *Fox News* shows and *Twitter*, which continued during his 2020 re-election campaign, until his Twitter account was banned

From over 1800 texts collected from the two leaders' statements and their news media coverage in the three selected periods, for the purposes of this study I closely analyzed a sample of over 100 "typical" texts. This sample was distributed in the following way: I analyzed three typical texts corresponding to each case study (Chávez and Trump) for each of the four variables and periods ($3 \times 2 \times 4 \times 3 = n72$); to this I added a minimum of three pieces of news media coverage ($3 \times 3 \times 2 = n18$). Together these texts formed the typical sample closely and critically analyzed in Chapter 5 ($72 + 18 = N100$). The analysis of the texts is qualitative and critical and was completed manually. I develop this analysis in a narrative and rather free or unstructured format in Chapter 5, which includes relevant quotations from the material and insights from academic, think tank, and news media commentators. For word limit reasons, I will only display three *typical* examples of Chávez's and Trump's speech performances and/or their respective coverage selected for their typicality, that is, for their salience or representativeness of each variable across the period.

The four-variable discursive disruption frame helps me evaluate Chávez's and Trump's respective communication styles as populist communicators vis-à-vis basic conventions of modern democracy, which I call the *indicators of discursive disruption*; this means that I assess the extent to which Chávez's and Trump's speech performances have indeed upset or unsettled democratic discourses prevailing in their respective countries before they rose to power; and in particular, whether their acts of discursive disruption led to intolerance, blockages or closure in the political dialogue, which might have had an impact on the polity and eventually, on the delegitimization of the system.

The analysis and discussion of Chávez's and Trump's speech performances will help me answer this study's main research questions, namely, are there any connections between the rise of populist communication and weakening democratic discourses due to discursive disruption? And, what are the main communicative strategies used by disruptive populist actors such as Chávez and Trump?

This study has limitations, mainly associated with the lack of a classic comparative study or empiricist quantification, which some scholars, depending on their discipline or approaches to the field, might find problematic. This study will nonetheless generate thick, critical, and specific descriptions and analyses of the two cases, which is exactly what this book intended. I will ultimately typify the main indicators and implications of discursive disruption, which in themselves embody a novel contribution to the political and populist communication fields.

References

Block, E., & Negrine, R. (2017). The populist communication style: Toward a critical framework. *International Journal of Communication*, *11*, 20.

Carroll, R. (2013, March 5). In the end, an awful manager. *The New York Times*. https://www.nytimes.com/2013/03/06/opinion/in-the-end-chavez-was-an-awful-manager.html

Deacon, D., Pickering, M., Murdock, G., & Golding, P. (2021). *Researching communications: A practical guide to methods in media and cultural analysis.* Bloomsbury Publishing.

Escalante-Block, E. (2018). Hugo Chávez's use of emotional appeals. *Comunicazione politica, 19*(1), 51–72.

Gill, T. (2016, October 17). Tim Gill: Trump-Chávez comparisons "Obscure much more than they illuminate." *WOLA*, Venezuelan Politics and Human Rights. https://venezuelablog.org/tim-gill-trump-chavez-comparisons-obscure-much/

Heinrich, J. (2007). *Thank you for arguing.* Random House.

Hymes, D. (1967). Models of the interaction of language and social setting. *Journal of Social Issues, 23*(2), 8–28. https://doi.org/10.1111/j.1540-4560.1967.tb00572.x

Hymes, D. (1972). Models of interaction of language and social life. In J. J. Gumperz, & D. Hymes (Eds.), *Directions in sociolinguistics: The ethnography of communication* (pp. 35–71). Holt: Rinehart & Winston.

Martin, J. (2013). *Politics and rhetoric: A critical introduction.* Routledge.

Meczkowski, E. J., & Dillard, J. P. (2017). Fear appeals in strategic communication. In P. Rössler, C. A. Hoffner, & L. van Zoonen (Eds.), *The international encyclopedia of media effects* (pp. 1–9). John Wiley & Sons.

R Foundation. (2018). *The R Project for Statistical Computing* (R version 4.1.0 Camp Pontanezen) [Computer software]. https://www.r-project.org/

Sartori, G. (2002). *Homo videns: La sociedad teledirigida.* Taurus.

Sclafani, J. (2018). *Talking Donald Trump. A sociolinguistic study of style, metadiscourse, and political identity.* Routledge.

Simpson, J. K. (2017). Appeal to fear in health care: Appropriate or inappropriate? *Chiropractic & Manual therapies, 25*(1), 1–10.

Smilde, D. (2016, November 6). Debates on the Hugo Chávez/Donald Trump comparison. *Venezuelan Politics and Human Rights.* https://venezuelablog.org/debate-on-the-hugo-chavez-donald-trump/

Thomas, G. (2011). A typology for the case study in social science following a review of definition, discourse, and structure. *Qualitative Inquiry, 17*(6), 511–521. https://doi.org/10.1177/1077800411409884

Van Leeuwen, T. (2007). Legitimation in discourse and communication. *Discourse & Communication, 1*(1), 91–112.

5 Chávez and Trump as paradigms of discursive disruption

> This aptness of language is one thing that makes people believe in the truth of your story; their minds draw the false conclusion that you are to be trusted...Besides, an emotional speaker always makes his audience feel with him, even when there is nothing in his arguments; which is why many speakers try to overwhelm their audiences by mere noise.
>
> (Aristotle, 347–367 B.C.E.)

In this fifth chapter, I test the discursive disruption analytical framework built in Chapter 4, through contrasting a set of Chávez's and Trump's typical texts against the four proposed variables, namely, (1) language; (2) identity; (3) use of and relationship with the media; and (4) acceptance or dismissal of the values, conventions, and discourses that have been associated with modern democracy. The fourth variable was broken down into three sets of subvariables exploring Chávez's and Trump's respect for: (a) democratic freedoms and rights; (b) separation of powers and rule of law; and (c) plural and rational dialogue and free and fair elections.

I study the two populist presidents' speech strategies. As Bolívar and Escudero (2021) argued, impolite antidemocratic discourses and language by significant political leaders seeking self-legitimation among likeminded audiences deserve deep and critical evaluation as "impoliteness has social, economic and political implications for the international dialogue" (p. 2). This argument leads to my first variable, the use of language.

5.1 Use of language

One of the main and most obvious traits of Chávez's and Trump's populist communication styles is their controversial use of an antidialogic, insulting language that polarizes audiences, builds bonds with

DOI: 10.4324/9781003118602-5

their loyal constituents, and exacerbates differences with their opponents and often constructed, custom built "enemies".

Álvarez and Chumaceiro (2011), specifically, defined insults as a "strong expression of intolerance, violence hidden in words, verbal assault on a person" (p. 1); speech acts that "intentionally harm the self-esteem of the person to whom it is directed. It involves contempt and mistreatment of the image of the other; it also produces offense by irritating, outraging or dishonoring its victim" (p. 1). Insult strategies use emotional appeals that connect with populist audiences and media as they trigger controversy and clickbait, cancel/hate/love comments, as well as shares by friends and foes.

Chávez became the bully-in-chief due to one of his most prominent stylistic tools, which was the normalization of insults in Venezuelan politics. Wittmeyer's (2013) work on what she called "The Bullyvarian Revolution" (p. 1) suggested that the numerous insults expressed by the President "with gusto" were a key component of his "brand of charisma" (para. 2). As Álvarez and Chumaceiro (2011) suggested, the insult can be an effective tactic to trigger "strategic conflict" with opponents and emotional bonding with followers, which confirms that populist players, such as Chávez, "not only seek to disqualify, aggravate and provoke the other, but even cancel them as an interlocutor" (p. 1). This foregoing discussion suggests that public insults express intolerance, "violence hidden in the word, verbal assault on a person" (Álvarez & Chumaceiro, 2011, p. 11), as insults not only hurt and shun the insulted but also tend to unsettle the mood of the political communication culture of the group or society in which they occur.

Chávez used ad hominem speech against those who dared to oppose him, from opposition leaders who little by little were weakened by his ongoing discursive abuse, to the influential heads of the Catholic Church, one of the few institutions that were still trusted in traditionally Catholic Venezuela. In 2007, during a constitutional referendum to decide the installation of his "21st Century Bolivarian Socialism", there were important opposition voices publicly alerting against Chávez's antidemocratic tendencies, one of which was the Catholic Church and, specifically, the late Cardinal Rosalio Castillo Lara, a prominent Vatican figure. The president called the cardinal a "hypocrite, bandit, the devil in a cassock" ("Fallece el Cardenal", 2007, para. 3). Later, in October the same year, a furious president expanded his insults against the Episcopal Conference and the Bishops at large, calling them an "embarrassment" and claiming, "They say that the Reform is morally unacceptable. They are the morally unacceptable, we are ashamed of those bishops that we have" (Chávez fustiga, 2007, para. 3).

Chávez lost the 2007 constitutional referendum, his only electoral defeat in 13 years in government. Chávez blamed the bishops, together with the media for this electoral loss. He never forgot or forgave. He wanted to impose his own brand of socialist populism in 2007. In December, a defeated but defiant, mercurial and swearing Chávez, told his opponents to calculate well how to manage their "shitty victory" or *"victoria de mierda"* ("Chávez Califica", 2007, para. 1). Chávez's intolerance and lack of disposition to dialogue or to work together with the winners were evident in these exchanges. The mood of the country continued to worsen, polarization became stronger; everyone was compelled to take a side, chavista or antichavista, with no possibility for middle positions. Centre ground individuals were viewed with distrust by the two extremes who refused to converse, give in or compromise. In 2010 he attacked the Catholic church again, adding the Pope and the Vatican to the mix, calling them "troglodyte" and "cavemen", and threatening with reviewing diplomatic agreements with the Vatican ("Chávez Arremete de Nuevo", 2010).

Chávez's insults and the rude way he represented his enemies were not only inconsistent with his alleged Christian beliefs but also with his alleged socialist and revolutionary values. His insults had no ideology or religion. In 2008, the president singled out the Communist Party of Venezuela as one his enemies because they did not merge with Chávez's newly founded unified "super-party", Partido Socialista Unido de Venezuela (PSUV), a gesture that the president never forgave. Defiantly, Chávez's publicly warned Communist party officials: "We have to make you disappear from the political map" ("Hugo Chávez Amenaza", 2008, para. 1)

Chávez was an authoritarian egocentric leader, who was especially sensitive to criticism by foreign leaders who had been increasingly concerned about his antidemocratic discourse, his disrespect for human rights, separation of powers, the rule of law and pluralism. These democratic principles have been compromised since the change of the Constitution in 2000, which although it had offered a "participative" democracy, it rather helped Chávez to progressively gain greater power by making the legislative, judicial, and electoral powers less independent. For example, when Mexico's former President Vicente Fox supported a failed US proposal to resuscitate the Free Trade Area of the Americas (FTAA), Chávez said to him in a pitiful tone, "How sad that the president of a people like the Mexicans lets himself become the puppy dog of the empire" ("Chávez and Fox

Dispute Escalates", 2005, para. 12). Adriana Bolívar's (2008) analysis of this discursive clash demonstrated the complexity and importance of "ideological, moral and cultural" undertones embodied in political insults. Mexico demanded an apology that was never offered by Chavez, which caused more bitter exchanges and withdrawal of both ambassadors. So verbal action, in this case, became material action.

When Hugo Chávez delivered a speech at the UN conference in 2006, he called George W. Bush "the devil" and "world dictator"; in a defiant tone he warned that many nations were rising against American imperialism, demanding equality, respect and the sovereignty of nations. Below are segments of the speech reproduced by *The New York Times'* correspondent David Stout (2006):

> Yesterday, the devil came here... And it smells of sulfur still today, this table that I am now standing in front of... Yesterday, ladies and gentlemen, from this rostrum, the president of the United States, the gentleman to whom I refer as the devil, came here, talking as if he owned the world. Truly. As the owner of the world".
>
> (para 2)

Branding critics "the devil" has been part of how Chávez, and also Trump, implemented the "demonization" of their respective opponents. Romero-Rodriguez and Römer-Pieretti (2016), have suggested that the preferential access that populist leaders, such as Hugo Chavez, have had to national and international platforms, such as the UN, provides them with the ideal megaphone to institutionalize and legitimize their versions of reality *through language.*

Jamieson and Taussig (2017) studied demonization, disruption, and norm-destruction strategies as "the rhetorical signature of Donald Trump" (p. 619). They considered irrational and sentimental elements of Trump's rhetoric that included "seeming spontaneity laced with Manichean evidence-flouting, accountability dodging, and institution disdaining claims" (p. 620), thus breaking with traditional discursive conventions that recommended a "sanitized, prepackaged rhetoric" (p. 620).

The discussion above suggests that norm disruption had increased the perception among populist audiences that their leader was not afraid of *calling things as they are,* which, I argue, is one of the most appealing discursive traits shared by Chávez and Trump. This further explains why Trump's and Chávez's loyal audiences have trusted them even if what they say lacks any logic or substantiation.

Like Chávez, Donald Trump also excelled in his use of ad hominem rhetoric, which maintained political and media audiences and ordinary people in a state of permanent outrage, but also in anticipation of what he was going to say next. Trump started insulting opponents and critics, or just anybody that did not look or think like him, early in his campaign in 2015, after launching his nomination. *CNN*'s Kopan (2015) documented that by then Trump had already attacked ten specific groups of people, namely, the disabled (by mocking them with gestures); journalists (by sparring publicly with former Fox anchor Megyn Kelly and Univison's reporter Jorge Ramos); Iowans (by putting them down); Muslims (threatening to shut some Mosques down); Seven-Day Adventists (by doubting them); African Americans (by accusing them of high murder rates using false statistics); Asians (by mocking their business talk); women (calling Hillary Clinton "shrill"); senator John McCain (saying he was not a war hero); and his opponents, calling former Florida Governor Jeb Bush "low energy," Senator Marco Rubio a "clown" and repeatedly disparaged Kentucky Senator Rand Paul's looks. Trump also accused Hillary Clinton of having fake hair and called Vermont Senator Bernie Sanders a "maniac" (Kopan, 2015, para. 14).

The New York Times's Kevin Quealy (2021) built a list of Trump's Twitter insults from 2015 until 2020, which "features thousands of entries and 850 individual targets" (van Syckle, 2021, para. 2) and highlights Trump's verbal, mediatized, aggression. These practices should not surprise anyone, as Trump is a media creature who knows that insults are newsworthy and boost clickbait.

There have also been multiple scholarly studies and news media reports about Trump's irrational, demagogical, insult-style rhetoric weaponized in rallies and, especially, on Twitter (see Fitzduff, 2017; Jamieson & Taussig, 2017; Mercieca, 2020; Sclafani, 2018; Winberg, 2017, among many others). In his study on Donald Trump's language, Winberg (2017) argued that although "negative campaigning" has been a fundamental part of American political history, as indeed it has been in Western politics, the term does not capture the accuracy, fairness, or appropriateness of some forms of campaign aggression. Particularly, it does not capture the polemic and offensive insult style of politics that has marked "the populist-fuelled ad hominem, attacks of Donald Trump" (Winberg, 2017, p. 3); Winberg (2017) explained that "insult politics" focuses on "ad hominem attacks of disparaging nature aimed at an individual or group" (p. 3), which he represents as one of the main ingredients of right-wing populism that uses a "norm breaking language" (p. 3).

His antagonistic stance against the National Football League (NFL) players, who "took a knee" during the US National Anthem, was controversial and widely discussed in the media. Trump's posture involved both a bullying and threatening rhetoric that was mixed with identity politics, race, and patriotism. *Patriotism* is one of the cue terms used by Trump's staunch supporter group QAnon which is a far-right, white, supremacist mainly online outlet, or cult, whose message is mainly based on antipolitical conspiracy theories (Roose, 2021). In 2016, significant NFL players started kneeling during the National Anthem played at the beginning of the games in protest about police brutality and racism. The players have been adamant about their right to protest. Trump found in them a new, very convenient vis-à-vis his base, kind of enemy. At a rally in Alabama, Trump called the players unpatriotic and disrespectful and publicly swore at them. Trump's audiences at the rally cheered the weaponization, abuse, and vulgarity of his words. *The Guardian's* Bryan Armen Graham (2017) reproduced some segments of Trump's speech as follows: "Wouldn't you love to see one of these NFL owners, when somebody disrespects our flag, to say, 'Get that son of a bitch off the field right now, out, he's fired. He's fired!'" (para.2). The weaponization of Trump's words was represented by Venezuelan cartoonist and visual artist Rayma Suprani in the political cartoon in Figure 5.1, part of her exhibition, "Amor in Tiempos de Trump", or in English, "Love in Times of Trump" (2017).

Figure 5.1 "Amor en tiempos de Trump" (2017)

Source: Courtesy of visual artist Rayma Suprani.

Like Chávez, Trump used the UN podium 10 years later to insult a carefully selected enemy, South Korean leader Kim Jong-un; Trump provided a dark vision of the world and demanded from the UN solutions for countries in crisis in a renewed albeit implicit criticism to the organization. He also sought to publicly exacerbate American patriotic feelings in populist style, through the use of the terms sovereignty and patriotism, terms that were equally massaged by Chávez domestically and internationally against "imperialist" domination. Trump (Full text, 2017) developed his UN 2017 speech in binary terms:

> If the righteous many do not confront the wicked few, then evil will triumph...The United States has great strength and patience, but if it is forced to defend itself or its allies, we will have no choice but to totally destroy North Korea. Rocket Man is on a suicide mission for himself and for his regime.
>
> (para. 35; 40)

The Washington Post's Philip Bump (2019) tallied that in his first two years in power, Trump had delivered his 32 favorite insults 1693 times to disparage 245 different targets (among people or organizations). "Fake" was the most common insult, which Trump had used more than 300 times mainly against the media. The second insult counted by Bump (2019) was "failed" or "failing", applied 205 times, mostly to *The New York Times*. He used the term "dishonest" 149 times, "weak" 94 times, and "lying" or "liar" 68 times. Other terms were "dope", "crazy", "nut job", "phony", and "disgraced"; and Trump applied 15 different insults to Hillary Clinton, among which "crooked Hillary" is perhaps the most memorable. Further, Trump started calling then candidate Joe Biden "Sleepy Joe". However, some commentators argue that this frame was not as sticky as "crooked Hillary" due to Biden's appeal (Pindell, 2020).

Similarly, in his last presidential campaign, when he already suffered from cancer, Chávez called opposition candidate, Henrique Capriles, several nicknames, such as "fascist", "corrupt", "little bourgeois boy", and, especially, "majunche" an idiosyncratic term that means mediocre ("Apodos e Insultos", 2012). Chávez used the term "squalid" to pejoratively name, frame and shame all the members of the opposition, a term that became normalized and even used by some in the same opposition to jokingly, or sometimes proudly, identify themselves. He also called his opponents "the oligarchy", or just the "right", framing the political debate in ideological terms, in the same way that Trump called Biden "a socialist" or even a communist, because he defended healthcare programs like Obamacare ("Trump Accuses", 2020).

Chávez, like Trump, constructed the opposition *discursively*, by unifying all his opponents under the same humiliating name. He also constructed his own followers discursively, as the "Bolivarian sovereign" people of Venezuela. Both presidents not only use the term "sovereign" to represent their respective countries and "the people", but also to exacerbate resentments against political elites by reinforcing their radical vision of the "forgotten" people of America, or Venezuela. This theme was the highlight of Trump's victory speech; he said, "The forgotten men and women of our country will be forgotten no longer." ("Here's the Full Text", 2016, para 11). Such discursive constructions of the people suggest the use of identity politics in power relations.

5.2 Construction of identity

In Chapter 3, I commented on Young's (1997) view of identity politics as the discourse to blame when democracy is eroded. She argued that the "blind loyalty" displayed by identity groups has led contemporary societies to clannish political environments, which, I argue, are now reinforced by some social media communities thriving on adversarial, often hateful discourses based on an ongoing manipulation of identity. Thus, Young's (1997) work shows how *language and identity meet* in some political, and especially populist discourses, which, whether intentionally or not, aspire to close the public conversation on certain identity and nationalistic issues.

Chávez's Bolivarian and Trump's "Make America Great Again" (MAGA) nationalistic and patriotic imaginaries are fundamental to their respective identity discourses. However, both Chávez and Trump manipulated other identity issues (poverty and social marginalization; antiestablishment sentiments, political disenchantment, religious, and cultural prejudices) at whim in the construction of their power.

The use of identity is at the heart of Chávez's and Trump's populist communication styles. They both focused their messages on giving an identity to the marginalized, the politically alienated, or disenchanted, the forgotten Venezuelans or Americans that had been neglected by the political or party elites. Identity politics is about constructing, positioning, and mobilizing likeminded people *discursively* in the political debate by feeding off nationalistic values, cultural, rational, and religious fears and prejudices, in a process that excludes those who do not think, act, or look like them.

Of course, due to obvious cultural, political, and socioeconomic discrepancies, the forgotten groups of Venezuela and the US looked very different. Whereas Trump's base was rather homogenous, mainly formed by white, anti-Washington elite, anti-immigration, blue collar, religious conservative, "boomer" generation peoples, as explained in Chapter 3, in Venezuela, Chávez's initial vote was formed by rather heterogenous groups that shared strong antipolitical elites' feelings. A first subgroup was formed by middle class, center-left voters who criticized the performance of traditional parties; also, by those who have been rejected somehow or did not benefit from those elites. The second subgroup was formed by low income and marginal groups who felt that they had been forgotten by democracy. Antipolitical feelings predated Chávez's Venezuela. Such feelings had been boosted by traditional parties' episodes of corruption and mismanagement, emerging and ambitious civil society leaders and political outsiders as well as news media narratives continuously condemning all politicians and politics at large (see Block, 2015).

Thus, both Chávez and Trump manipulated identity profusely and intentionally. Their antagonistic discourse served the triple purpose of mobilizing their base, create controversy and build identity. Römer Pieretti (2014, p. 56) argued that Chávez made a "discursive and mediatic" manipulation of ancestral values and imaginaries that had been typical of the least favored races within the Spanish colonial caste system (black, indigenous, and mestizos). Chávez managed to transform Venezuelan identity politically and culturally through thriving on narratives and prejudices that little by little had been blurred over 200 years since Independence. Römer Pieretti (2014) called this new imaginary "*la venezolanidad chavista*" (p. 56), which in English could be translated as "chavista Venezuela". It was a top-down reshaped identity built by Chávez for power purposes.

In his 1998 pre-inauguration speech, Chávez, a former lieutenant colonel or commandant, began to shape his personal brand of identity politics. He said,

> I am a little of all of you...You will guide the government that will not be Chávez's government! Because Chávez is the people! It will be the government of the people! ...I, Hugo Chávez, do not belong to myself ... All my being belongs to you, the Venezuelan people. You are the owners of Venezuela's future.
> (Discurso de Proclamacion, 1998, p.23).

Then, in January 1999, in his official inauguration,

> This spiritual rebirth, this idea of national identity, this idea of who we are, of awareness of our being, of that self-esteem about

which so much has been spoken of in the last years.... So now, lift your self-esteem, lift your spirits, lift your morale! We are Venezuela, men, women, young and children, one of the most glorious people in history.

(Chávez, 1999a, para. 24).

Chávez's identity narratives built across his 13-year rule. I characterized 2012, his last year in government, as the year of "mimetization", a process that describes what happens when the bond built between the populist leaders with his followers is so strong that these fanatic audiences claimed that they *were* Chávez (Block, 2015). The following text illustrates the way Chávez represented this event: "I am not longer Chávez! Chávez is the people! Chávez, we are millions.... You are also Chávez...Because Chávez is not me anymore, Chávez is the people!" (Chávez, 2012, as cited in Block, 2015, pp. 218–219).

Chávez won the 2012 election and died of cancer in March 2013. Block (2015) described an interview with one of the members of one of the chavista *"colectivos"* (community power groups, often armed and politically influential in poor or popular areas). At his headquarters, the leader of the *colectivo* told me that Chávez made them feel empowered, and aware of who they are and who is 'the other'. Chávez "gave us an identity" (Block, 2015, p. 18), he said. However, I argue, a top down, discursively constructed identity, which was *Chávez's own.*

Donald Trump also used his inauguration to construct the identity of his constituents and enemies, a task he had already started in 2015 in his nomination acceptance speech at the Republican National Convention in Cleveland. The news media documented an electric atmosphere dominated by fanatic followers' chanting "Lock her up" ("Donald Trump: I am", 2016, para. 5), referring, of course, to Hillary Clinton. Trump had offered to take his Democratic opponent to prison for the notorious email scandal. He also situated some of the main themes of his campaign and presidency, such as "America First" and building "'the wall" (at the Mexico border), and represented himself as the law-and-order candidate. He also constructed some of his enemies, namely, the "political status quo" ("Donald Trump: I am", 2016, para. 14), immigrants, Muslim terrorists, and former president Obama, who, Trump claimed, "divided us by race and color" (para. 19). There were some lines in Trump's speech that made some Venezuelans experience an uncanny déjà vu, "I'm with you, the American people: I am your voice" ("Donald Trump: I am", 2016, para. 10).

Trump's inauguration speech was directly targeted to his base, a group of Americans who, according to Norris and Inglehart (2019), felt that conservative morals and traditional values should return as they feared the liberal changes taking place in American life; these authors also documented some surveys that registered an increase in anti-immigration and pro-authoritarian feelings notably among the younger generation.

In his inaugural speech, Trump set a dividing line between the people and the evil members of the establishment:

> For too long, a small group in our nation's capital has reaped the rewards of government, while the people have borne the cost. Washington flourished, but the people did not share in its wealth. Politicians prospered, but the jobs left and the factories closed. The establishment protected itself, but not the citizens of our country. Their victories have not been your victories…
> ("Full Text: 2017 Donald Trump Inauguration", 2017, para 4)

Trump used again the term "forgotten" and expanded his construction of *the people*, his loyal constituents:

> The forgotten men and women of our country will be forgotten no longer. Everyone is listening to you now…Today's ceremony, however, has a very special meaning because today we are not merely transferring power from one administration to another or from one party to another, but we are transferring power from Washington, D.C., and giving it back to you, the people…
> ("Full Text: 2017 Donald Trump Inauguration", 2017, para. 4)

Trump's identity politics triggered protests and demonstrations every year and nearly every month of his four years in the presidency, mobilized in the US and other countries by domestic and international movements, equally driven by identity politics but of another kind, as these rejected Trump's bigoted, misogynistic, racist, pro-gun, anticlimate change views.

At a press conference also in 2017 but 7 months later, the president defended the controversial Charlottesville rally, led by white supremacists, ultra-nationalists and alleged Neo-Nazis; Trump defiantly defended the rally saying that it was important to hear "both sides", as "many people … other than neo-Nazis and white nationalists" have been treated "absolutely unfairly" (Nelson & Swanson, 2017, para. 2).

Four years later, on January 6, 2021, Trump used identity politics again in his so called "Save America" rally, this time to steer, or incite, his "Big Lie" supporters just a few hours before the Capitol Hill insurrection. Trump situated the conflict in antagonistic, World Wrestling Entertainment (WWE) terms, weaponizing his MAGA ideology as a struggle between the American patriots versus the radical left democrats:

> ...Hundreds of thousands of American patriots are committed to the honesty of our elections and the integrity of our glorious Republic. All of us here today do not want to see our election victory stolen by emboldened radical left Democrats, which is what they're doing and stolen by the fake news media....We will never give up. We will never concede, it doesn't happen. You don't concede when there's theft involved.
>
> ("Donald Trump Speech 'Save'", 2021, para. 1)

The January 6 speech showed the power of Trump's words to incite and disrupt the masses, and democracy, getting news media's attention in the process. This specific illustration demonstrated the power of words to boost material action. These events were the cause of his second impeachment by Congress, the first president to get impeached twice, in what he has called a "witch hunt". Trump had never wanted or meant to concede peacefully, he did, and still does, aim to dominate and disrupt the political and media agenda, no matter the logic or implications of his remarks. In Aristotle's (1984) terms (see this chapter's epigraph), Trump uses "mere noise" to distract and *overwhelm* political and media spaces.

The media was positioned as the permanent enemy in Trump's, and also Chávez's, discursive games.

5.3 Use of and relationship with the media

Chávez and Trump have been expert media operators that know how to effectively use all forms of media, both, traditional news media and social media, to construct and maintain identity and power. Most of their speech performances have been destined to increase controversy, conflict, and confrontational politics of the spectacle that boost headlines and clickbait. They both were aware that political bullying and impoliteness were attractive to news media outlets that are always eager for scandal and spectacle-style politics (Bolívar & Escudero, 2021). Chávez has been represented as the "ultimate showman" (McCarthy, 2013) and Trump as the "first reality TV president" (Nesbit, 2016, para. 1). Their populist leaderships grew and throve on media, even, or perhaps especially when they were attacked. They were able to define the media's agenda through what Bracho-Polanco (2020), in his study of Chávez, called a "hyper-mediatic" leadership. Leaders like Chávez (and I would add Trump) seek to represent and legitimize themselves as "popular" to dominate the news agenda. Bracho-Polanco (2020, p. 48) interviewed a group of journalists who confirmed that Chávez indeed managed "to establish an important portion of the news agenda" though his TV shows.

Trump also dominated the global media's agenda. Tilley et al. (2017) studied the mention of the name "Trump" in US cable for a few months after his 2017 inauguration; their results showed that in just 19 days of the period studied he is mentioned more than 50% of the broadcast time on two of the networks, *MSNBC* and *CNN*, his main archenemies from the American so called "liberal" or left media. This confirms that populists like Trump, and also Chávez, fed on media outrage. The same networks Trump repeatedly called "Fake news" (particularly MSNBC and CNN) provided media outrage on a 24/7 basis. The same phenomenon happened with Chávez and Globovisión, the cable and over-the-air news network that became Chávez's nemesis throughout his rule (now in the hands of a pro-chavista business group). Globovisión even created a daily talk show called *Aló Ciudadano*, in 2002 as an extreme counterpart to Chávez's Aló Presidente (1999). This show, which lasted until Chávez died in 2013 (Castillo, 2013), in some ways substituted, and also rather obscured, the role of opposing political parties in the debate.

Media-leader clashes help increase a leader's popularity. For example, Professor Jeff Jarvis told David Sillito (2016) that by covering Trump's irrational outbursts and continuously wrestling with him, the media had given Trump "a free pass" (para. 16). In this regard, Rosenberg (2019) discussed Stephan Lewandowsky's study which provided quantitative evidence not only for the distraction caused by Trump's tweets, but that "the media respond[ed] to the distraction by reducing their coverage of the threatening theme that triggered the distraction in the first place" (para. 31), in this case, the Muller probe. This claim is consistent with Lakoff's (2017) classification of Trump's tweets in terms of pre-emptive framing (being the first to frame and often shame): diversion, deflection, and trial balloons.

Both Trump and Chávez have been savvy social media operators that understood how to engage with their audiences. Bickart et al. (2017) listed a series of social media techniques that Trump used, such as publishing memorable, controversial content; using Twitter in a personal not presidential way to create a direct relationship with

his audiences thus bypassing news media moderation (although eventually Trump could not avoid platform moderation and even banning
or cancellation); these authors claimed that such messages sought to
"gain traction through the power of provocation", and to "polar-
ize, alienate and enflame" (para. 12). The same argument could be
applied to analyze Chávez's use of social media. After considering it
a tool for terrorism, Chávez embraced Twitter in April 2010, as a tool
"to fight online conspiracy of the opposition from within" (Carroll,
2010, para. 1). Chávez said that Twitter and Blackberry were his
new "secret weapons" of war. His handle @Chavezcandanga had 4
million followers by March 2013 when he died. Chávez weaponized
Twitter in the same way he weaponized Aló Presidente (1999) and his
national "chains" of radio and TV (a mandatory state mechanism
that compelled all networks to transmit presidential messages that in
the case of Chávez lasted up to 5 or 6 hours), using them to insult and
threaten opponents and journalists alike and even to abuse or fire his
own ministers. Chávez maintained a permanent confrontation with
the commercial media, threatening media owners and journalists,
and eventually fulfilling the threat by not renewing their licenses,
expropriating, or closing some of the main commercial TV and radio
networks; between 2007 and 2009, RCTV was terminated, along with
245 radio networks and 45 regional TV channels (Vinogradoff, 2009).
This demonstrated that Chávez's aim for communicational hegemony was becoming a reality.

Moreover, Chavez's insults to journalists became normalized. He
rudely called Radio France's correspondent Andreina Flores "igno-
rant" in front of the cameras (Así Ataca, 2011); she said that she con-
stantly felt "threatened, watched". Most democratic presidents have
clashes with the media, as this is part of the democratic game; however,
journalists should not be intimated, bullied, threatened, or banned by
a president.

Trump's use of traditional news media not only consisted of his
experience as a reality show presenter on NBC's "The Apprentice"
(n.d.), and through his appearances on right-wing *Fox News*. Trump
tried to restrict the access of the news media to government barring
journalists from major media outlets from press briefings, notably
CNN, The New York Times, Politico, BuzzFeed, and most of the
foreign press (Golshan, 2017). Trump lashed journalists publicly by
naming and shaming them on live TV, as an intimidation strategy
to boost fear and outrage within the same media. At the heart of
these acts was that Trump, like Chávez, demonstrated zero tolerance to criticism or uncomfortable questions. He controversially

removed White House credentials for *CNN*'s Jim Acosta who asked Trump uncomfortable questions about immigration and the Muller investigation into Russian interference in the 2016 elections, which led to *CNN* suing Trump's administration for violating Acosta's First Amendment rights (Grynbaum, 2018). But Trump's most vicious attacks were addressed to female journalist's especially women, particularly women of color. He did it through chauvinistic stereotypes, "reducing women to their looks or their intellect" (Phillips, 2018, para. 5).

After Trump was banned from Twitter and other social media outlets, he created his own blog (to continue bypassing the moderation of the news media), which had little success, suggesting he had made Twitter a powerful and disruptive political tool. A blog does not have the same punch.

During their presidential periods both Chávez and Trump were under the continuous scrutiny of multilateral, global, and regional organizations and think tanks, such as The United Nations Commission for Human Rights, Amnesty International, Freedom House, and Human Rights Watch (some of these studies were cited and used in Chapter 3). Their annual reports substantiated that both presidents intimidated, retaliated, and discriminated against media that published their opponents' views, aiming at what Lugo-Ocando and Cañizalez (2021) called "media Caesarism". Chávez and Trump hegemonically controlled the media by dominating the agenda; and in the case of Chávez, by eliminating media licenses, and creating a restrictive environment in which traditional news media could not thrive. This raises the question of whether, with more time in the White House and the submissive attitude of a significant faction of the Republican Party, Trump also could have reached a level of media Caesarism. What he did arguably achieve was to disrupt and darken the media conversation. Both presidents saw the media as their true opposition, branded the media as "the enemy of the people" and called them "fake" or liars. The mediatization and polarization of politics and the politicization and polarization of the media reined in Chávez's Venezuela and Trump's US. They both used the media against the same media.

Chávez's attacks against the media raged in 2006, the year of his second presidential election (under the new constitution). He announced, "I have ordered the review of the concessions of the television networks" ("Chávez Ordena", 2006). In 2007, Chávez revoked the RCTV's concession, the largest and oldest TV network, with 53 years on air. This decision triggered marches and protests and domestic and international outrage. In a defiant, authoritarian tone that decreed closure without any possibility of dialogue, the president announced:

> They better go packing and see what they are going to do as of March because the broadcasting license for this coup-plotting TV channel that used to be called Radio Caracas Televisión will not be renewed!... This is over!.
>
> ("Chávez revocará", 2006, para. 1-3)

As I noted earlier, in 2009, the year of the constitutional referendum that would grant him the possibility of "indefinite reelections", Chávez increased his attacks on the media, calling them "conspirators" that "trample the truth and incite war" ("Chávez, Contra", 2009, para. 1). The Inter-American Press Association accused Chávez "of inciting, through his criticisms, attacks against the press such as those experienced by reporters from the Globovision" ("Chávez, Contra", 2009, para. 1). However, he did not end the license of Globovision, as he did with RCTV, possibly because he needed the sparring but less powerful partner to distract and deflect attention.

Donald Trump could not have closed TV networks, *yet*, but slammed the media on an everyday basis. Early in his presidency, after he was inaugurated on 17 February 2017, Trump wrote on Twitter, "The FAKE NEWS media (failing @newyorktimes, @CNN, @NBCNews, and many more) is not my enemy, it is the enemy of the American people. SICK" (Trump, 2017a)

This tweet marked his stormy relationship with the media during his presidency. Trump's media raids became normalized. Demonizing a person by calling them enemy of the people is not new and is destined to close any "ideological fight". As Higgins (2017) noted, former soviet prime minister Nikita Khrushchev demanded the end of the use of this term that was connected with Stalin's cult of personality to justify the physical annihilation of individuals who "disagreed with the supreme leader" (para. 2)

Later, on 12 May the same year, Trump threatened in a tweet to cancel press briefings: "Q1: 'Maybe the best thing to do would be to cancel all future 'press briefings' and hand out written responses for the sake of accuracy???'" (Trump, 2017b).

In October 2017, in a Tweet that evoked Chávez's RCTV announcement, he said, "Network news has become so partisan, distorted and fake that licenses must be challenged and, if appropriate, revoked. Not fair to public!" (Trump, 2017c). Adding later the same day, in another Tweet, "With all of the Fake News coming out of NBC and the

Networks, at what point is it appropriate to challenge their License? Bad for country!" (Trump, 2017d).

Trump constructed the media as the enemy of the American people, not his personal enemy. A Hill-Harris Poll published in 2019 indicated that one third of Americans believed that the media is indeed the enemy, while 67% said that it is important for democracy (Lardieri, 2019). Trump had reached over 88 million Twitter followers when he was banned from the platform on January 8, 2021, due to "due to the risk of further incitement of violence" (Twitter Inc, 2021, para. 1). He used to tweet on average 5.7 times a day in the first half of his government, which increased to 34.8 times a day in 2020 (McCarthy, 2021). This intense messaging evokes, somehow, the feistiness with which Chávez handled his TV shows, sometimes on air for 8 hours in a row (Carroll, 2007). It was really, as Carroll (2007) put it referring to Chávez, government by TV, which in Trump's case could be called government by Twitter. The political conversation was interrupted and at times closed as no civil democratic dialogue could thrive in such disruptive, defiant, and conflictive environment.

5.4 Adherence or not to traditional democratic discourses

I will display next some of Chávez's and Trump's speech performances vis-à-vis the discourses and conventions of traditional democracy. Because of the complexity and number of the variables involved in the analysis, as well as word limit restrictions, I have grouped them into sets of texts (that include some typical speeches, statements and/or policy changes.). As explained earlier, these texts are grouped as follows: (a) adherence to freedoms, civil rights, and social justice; (b) separation of powers and rule of law; (c) respect for plural and rational dialogue and free and fair elections. The relationships of both Chávez and Trump with the constitution of their countries have been controversial and seem to bear some resemblances. For example, in his first inauguration in 1999, Chávez broke with the pledge repeated by every president during 40 years of democracy, "in front of my people that over this moribund constitution I will push forward the democratic transformations that are necessary so that the new republic will have an adequate Magna Carta for the times". (Tribune News Service, 1999, para. 3).

Trump's main problem with the Constitution and other laws established within the US's check and balances system is that they placed limits on his presidential power. In an interview with *Fox News*, which marked the first 100 days of his presidency, he claimed that the whole

American system of government is "a very rough system, an archaic system", adding that "it's a really bad thing for the country" (Fox News, 2017, para. 15–16).

Diverse international think tanks and nongovernmental international watchdogs or multilateral organizations, such as Freedom House, Amnesty International, Human Rights Watch, UN Commission for Human Rights, and Inter-American Commission of Human Rights (IACHR), among others, have reported Chávez's and Trump's problematic relationships with democratic conventions. In their annual reports these agencies have provided relevant data that have explained how Chávez and Trump contributed to the erosion, disruption, and even the end (in the case of Venezuela) of the democratic system that existed before they rose to power.

In the case of Hugo Chávez, his lack of adherence to discourses and conventions of democracy were well documented by human rights and democracy watchdog organizations mentioned above, particularly the IACHR.

Chávez despised the Constitution of 1961, which had lasted 40 years and consecrated representative democracy and a consensus system between the main political parties. Once he won his first presidential election in 1998, Chávez promoted the Constitutional Assembly that would draft the new carta magna. He took advantage of his popularity then to guarantee success. Thus, although he despised the representative democracy system, it was the same system that had served to elect him as a president. As a former military officer who had attempted a coup in 1992, Chávez had been at odds with democracy for a long time; he wanted to seize power by force, but he could not at this time, as he went to prison for 2 years. When he was pardoned, he still intended to take power but this time as a presidential candidate in democratic elections under a system that he despised. After achieving his first aim, to change the constitution and political system, he started to become more confrontational and intolerant of opponents. He rejected pluralism and criticism alike. As his victory had weakened and diminished the main political parties, in 2002 he started targeting other groups, mainly business and industry figures and, as noted earlier, the Catholic Church hierarchy. However, the commandant's fast move toward socialism and his attacks against civil society and religious institutions took Chávez to his lowest popularity moment; Venezuelans were not reacting positively to the depth and severity of the changes he wanted to complete.

Against this landscape, a significant sector of the opposition (mainly nontraditional parties, civil society, business and leading industry figures) also had their "at odds" disruptive and also rather clumsy moment against the constitution, as they attempted a coup (in the name of rescuing democracy) that succeeded for just 48 hours, as Chávez was reinstated the following day. The IACHR (2003) condemned the coup.

The business elite, that also included powerful news media groups, had felt threatened as Chávez, using special powers (granted by a chavista majority Congress) issued a 49-law package that affected their economic interests. The division and polarization of the country deepened, and it became impossible to find a political middle ground. Positions had to be taken for or against Chávez. The opposition attempted a Recall Referendum in 2004 that Chávez won; the opposition called these results a fraud, a thesis that was later supported by academic research (see Febres-Cordero and Marquez, 2006). After the failure in the Recall Referendum, the main remaining opposition parties abstained to participate in subsequent elections and encouraged voters to abstain.

In 2012, the year of Chávez's last presidential elections, when he already has been in power for 13 years, Human Rights Watch (2012) published a comprehensive report that documented Chávez's clashes with democracy and how human rights and freedoms had been affected during his years in government. The report stated that Chávez's concentration of powers has "taken a heavy toll on human rights in Venezuela" (para. 1). Relevantly, the report added that the Chavista majority in the National Assembly passed legislation that reinforced the regime's powers to limit free speech and punish its critics, adding that in 2010 the Supreme Tribunal of Justice was packed with Chávez's supporters, which ended any vestige of separation of powers and any possibility of presidential accountability in Venezuela.

Some of the most violent events were triggered or incited by Chávez's words. The media perhaps, was one of the most affected groups. Journalists were the target of Chávez's discursive aggression which incited radical chavista groups not only to reproduce verbal abuse but also to exert physical and material attacks on reporters and media property.

Since 2002, the same Human Rights Watch (2002) had exhorted Chávez to moderate his aggressive language that according to their report was inciting his followers to violence; "Given the polarized political situation, his critical statements may be read by his supporters as incitement to violence against the media" (para. 10).

Maingon and Welsch (2009) summarized the situation by suggesting that Chávez's regime was characterized by an increasingly weak rule

of law; disrespect for human rights, freedom of expression and information; rejection of pluralism; and significant number of complaints
lodged at international courts of justice for violations of human rights
of politicians and journalists, according to reports by IACHR, NGOs,
Provea, and Human Rights Watch (p. 634).

From 2002 onwards, separation of powers was further debilitated as
Chávez bypassed the legislative and judiciary systems using enabling
laws and special powers to govern and impose policy. Chávez never
believed in separation of powers, independence of the judiciary, or the
legislative processes. His view of separation of powers is explained in
one of his blogs written in 2009, a month after he was granted the possibility of indefinite reelection and he felt stronger and supported. The
fragment below is an illustration of how Chávez (2009) used words to
mobilize his followers against separation of powers:

> It is a great undeniable truth that walks the streets and in the voice
> of our compatriots: Here now there is a government! But this is
> not enough if we want to have a Republic: the time is ripe for all
> powers, freed from the burden of their division—as a consequence
> of a disastrous inheritance that we must overcome sooner rather
> than later—to work in coordination as required by popular con-
> stitutionalism that takes form in Venezuela and in Our America.
> The day must come when the voice of the people can say with full
> certainty: Now we do have a State!
>
> (para. 8)

Vote suppression and gerrymandering are not exclusive of the US or
other Western countries: Venezuela's Chávez had his own versions. In
reality it was not for lack of electoral processes, but maybe for the excessive number of elections of all types that deflected attention, boosted
voters' exhaustion, and increased distrust in electoral transparency that
both prevented people from participating in elections and made it easier
for Chávez to stay in power for so long. As electoral watchdog FairVote
("Hugo Chavez Electoral", 2009) indicated that Chavez compelled the
National Assembly "to alter the nation's electoral laws. Previously, 60%
of seats in the National Assembly were elected from single and mul-
ti-member districts by plurality vote while the remaining 40% were cho-
sen from proportional party lists. Now, the ratio will be respectively
70% and 30%... (para. 1). Naturally, these changes made the system less
proportional and more cumbersome for smaller parties

Hugo Chávez had 13 years to build power, identity, and autocracy
in Venezuela for himself and his successors (namely, Nicolas Maduro,

and his clique). Chávez progressively defaced Venezuelan politics through his antagonistic, intolerant and insulting discourse, multiple elections and referenda, and constitutional changes. The increasing dire economic situation and power, food, and water shortages, deflected people's attention from the enormity of the political events that were happening around them.

Trump just had 4 years in power and could not enact the political changes that he would have wanted. This is probably why he could not believe or fathom that he lost the 2020 election. As a businessman with an autocratic, rather narcissistic personality, Trump had been used to having his own way. He needed a second period to complete his disruptive task. However, from his conflictive relationship with Constitutions at the beginning of his government, to the incitation of the January 6 insurrection, all suggested that Trump, like Chávez, did not care for the discourses or convention of democracy, for example, he struggled with the concept of separation of powers throughout his years in the White House. As Suk (2020) argued, conservative Brett Kavanaugh's appointment as Supreme Court Justice was a step forward in Trump's path to try to block the examination of his conduct "by claiming that the chief executive is immune from various forms of investigation" (para. 10). Suk (2020) added that what was at stake then was "the public's ability to know about, and seek accountability for, misconduct. But, more important, they represent a gut check for our system of separation of powers" (para 1).

According to *The New York Times*' Charlie Savage (2020), Trump really believed he had the "ultimate authority", a claim that does not have any constitutional or legal foundation in the US. This outburst occurred at the height of the pandemic's lockdowns. Trump wanted to reopen the country by exerting imaginary special presidential powers. The next text explains he could not do this:

> President Trump's claim that he wielded "total" authority in the pandemic crisis prompted rebellion not just from governors. Legal scholars across the ideological spectrum on Tuesday rejected his declaration that ultimately, he, not state leaders, will decide when to risk lifting social distancing limits in order to reopen businesses.
> (Savage, 2020, para. 1)

But this attitude should not have surprised commentators in 2020. American Independent's Tommy Christopher (2017) reported at the very beginning of Trump's presidency, Trump's Director of Speechwriting, Steven Miller, had said on Face the Nation that

"Trump's power exceeded that of the judiciary, the people of the Unites States, the free press, or anyone else" (para. 4). Christopher (2017) also documented that on another show on *CBS*, Miller had added:

> The end result of this, though, is that our opponents, the media, and the whole world will soon see, as we begin to take further actions, that the powers of the president to protect our country are very substantial and will not be questioned
>
> (as cited in Christopher, 2017, para. 6)

Miller, as Trump's long-lasting senior speechwriter, embodies the intolerant, antipluralist, and antidialogic essence of Trump's presidency. Another example of Trump's intolerance toward separation of powers occurred later the same year, in May 2017, when he wanted to scrap Obamacare and cut taxes and Congress was preventing him from achieving this aim. The president then demanded in a Tweet, "The U.S. Senate should switch to 51 votes, immediately, and get Healthcare and TAX CUTS approved, fast and easy. Dems would do it, no doubt!" (Trump, 2017c).

He then threatened a government shutdown. He also wanted to end the filibuster as it was becoming an annoying stone in his shoe. *The Washington Post*'s Aaron Blake (2017, para. 1), documented the process:

> Update: Trump is indeed going ahead with a push to get rid of the filibuster, tweeting that the GOP should consider it if it can't get 60 votes to overcome the filibuster. He apparently even threatened to allow a government shutdown to prove his point.

Human Rights Watch (2021) in their report about events that occurred in the US in 2020, the first year of the COVID-19 pandemic, expressed their concern for Trump's continuation of attacks on news outlets and "questioned his administration policies" (p. 9). Also, for the way he threatened to retaliate against Twitter and other social media platforms that had added a fact-check label on his tweets, by seeming to "remove legal protections" (p. 9), which meant an attack "against freedom of expression globally" (p. 9). Human Rights Watch (2021) also expressed preoccupation for the way the president "took aggressive action against protesters demanding racial justice, particularly, sending federal officers to Portland despite questions about their authority to take enforcement action" (p. 9), which culminated in the use of excessive force. This watchdog organization also expressed concern for the government's steps toward voter suppression in primary elections during the pandemic.

Although Trump's mail ballot and the US Postal Service's rejection and fraud discourses are part of a long history of voter suppression, especially against black voters, this became a presidential obsession of Trump's own power game, which, simultaneously managed to hurt his own party's vote (Rubin, 2020).

More concentrated on acts that disrespected democracy, Freedom House (2021) indicated that Trump's "continual volleys of fraud allegations" (para. 10), which focused on states won by President Joe Biden led Trump's campaign staff and lawyers to intimidate mostly Republican election officials "regardless of the facts and the law." (para. 10). The "Big Lie" discourse, aided by online conspiracy theories, was taking shape and already winning the hearts and minds among Trump's blind followers despite the irrationality that underpinned such discourse. "Evidence of large-scale fraud was nonexistent, as the Justice Department eventually acknowledged despite pressure from the president". (Freedom House, 2021, para. 10)

The foregoing discussion shows how both Chávez and Trump used language and media: (a) to insult their opponents and anyone that dared criticize or block their decisions or intentions; (b) to construct the identity of their constituents as the forgotten "sovereign" and that of their opponents as "the enemy of the people" in an ad hominem, antagonistic style; (c) to display a brutal and savvy use of all forms of media and a conflictive relationship with journalists; and (d) to attempt to impose their antidemocratic, autocratic and antiplural agenda, transgressing the discourses and conventions of the democracy that predated their rise to power. Their speech performances *disrupted democracy within* democracy to pursue their own power purposes.

References

Aló Presidente. (1999). Hugo Chávez's TV show. http://www.alopresidente.gob.ve/historia/28/1633

Álvarez, A., & Chumaceiro, I. (2011). Insulto e intolerancia: La confrontación en el macro diálogo político. *Preconceito e intolerância: re exões linguístico-discursivas*, 137–176.

Apodos e insultos, táctica de campaña de Hugo Chávez. (2012, August 15). *El Universo*. https://www.eluniverso.com/2012/08/15/1/1361/apodos-insultos-tactica-campana-hugo-chavez.html

Armen Graham, B. (2017, September 24). Donald Trump blasts NFL anthem protesters; 'Get that son of a bitch off the field'. *The Guardian*. https://www.theguardian.com/sport/2017/sep/22/donald-trump-nfl-national-anthem-protests

Aristotle. (1984). *Complete works of Aristotle: The revised Oxford translation 2.* (J. Barnes, Ed.). Princeton University Press.

Así ataca Chávez a la prensa. (2011, November 3). *El País.* https://elpais.com/internacional/2011/11/03/actualidad/1320318293_144442.html

Bickart, B., Fournier, S., & Nisenholtz, M. (2017, March 1). What Trump understands about using social media to drive attention. *Harvard Business Review.* https://hbr.org/2017/03/what-trump-understands-about-using-social-media-to-drive-attention

Blake, A. (2017, May 2). Trump wants more power and fewer checks and balances—again. *The Washington Post.* https://www.washingtonpost.com/news/thefix/wp/2017/04/29/trump-is-now-talking-about-consolidating-his-own-power/

Block, E. (2015). *Political communication and leadership. Mimetization, Hugo Chávez and the construction of power and identity.* Routledge.

Bolívar, A. (2008). Cachorro del imperio" versus "cachorro de fidel": Los insultos en la política latinoamericana. *Discurso & Sociedad, 2*(1), 1–38.

Bolívar, A., & Escudero, A. (2021). la descortesía de Donald Trump hacia los migrantes mexicanos y la respuesta de la jornada en sus editoriales: La descortesía como práctica política. *Pragmática Sociocultural, 9*(1), 1–25. https://doi.org/10.1515/soprag-2021-0004

Bracho-Polanco, E. (2020). Chávez's aló presidente and its impact on Venezuela's journalistic practice. *Iberoamericana–Nordic Journal of Latin American and Caribbean Studies, 49*(1).

Bump, P. (2019). The expansive, repetitive universe of Trump's Twitter insults. *The Washington Post.* https://www.washingtonpost.com/politics/2019/08/20/expansive-repetitive-universe-trumps-twitter-insults/

Carroll, R. (2007, September 25). Government by TV: Chávez sets 8-hour record. *The Guardian.* https://www.theguardian.com/media/2007/sep/25/venezuela.television

Carroll, R. (2010, April 28). Hugo Chávez embraces Twitter to fight online conspiracy. The Guardian (online edition). http://www.theguardian.com/world/2010/apr/28/hugo-chavez-twitter-venezuela

Castillo, L. (Presenter). (2013, August 16). *Leopoldo Castillo: Me voy sin ninguna tristeza en el alma, la vida hará que nos crucemos de nuevo* [Video file]. http://globovision.com/seccion/editorial-alo-ciudadano/

Chávez, H. (1999a, February 2). *Inauguration Address: Hugo Chávez.* [Transcript]. http://www.analitica.com/bitblioteca/hchavez/toma.asp

Chávez, H. (2009, December 15). Del Mercosur al Alba. *Las Lineas de Chávez.* https://rebelion.org/del-mercosur-al-alba/

Chávez and Fox dispute escalates. (2005, November 15). *BBC News.* http://news.bbc.co.uk/2/hi/americas/4438876.stm

Chávez arremete de nuevo contra el Papa y el vaticano. (2010, July 15). *BBC News.* https://www.bbc.com/mundo/america_latina/2010/07/100715_chavez_iglesia_papa_vaticano_lr

Chávez califica de 'victoria de mierda' el triunfo de la oposición (2007, December 6). *El Mundo.* https://www.elmundo.es/elmundo/2007/12/06/internacional/1196897757.html

Chávez, contra medios "conspiradores". (2009, May 10). *BBC News.* https://www.bbc.com/mundo/america_latina/2009/05/090510_2300_chavez_hectareas_med

Chávez fustiga a los obispos por criticas a la reforma constitucional (2007, October 10). *Vocero Bolivariano.* http://vocerobolivariano.blogspot.com/2007/10/chvez-fustiga-obispos-por-crticas.html

Chávez ordena revisar las concesiones de televisión privada en Venezuela. (2006, June 15). *El Mundo.es.* https://www.elmundo.es/elmundo/2006/06/15/comunicacion/1150362475.html

Chávez revocará concesión a RCTV (2006, December 29). *El Tiempo.* https://www.eltiempo.com/archivo/documento/MAM-2330534

Christopher, T. (2017, February 12). In despotic declaration, Trump senior advisor says Trump's power 'will not be questioned'. *American Independent.* https://americanindependent.com/in-despotic-declaration-trump-senior-advisor-says-trumps-power-will-not-be-questioned/

Discurso de Proclamación del Comandante Presidente Electo Hugo Chávez por el Consejo Nacional Electoral. (1998, December, 14). http://www.todochavezenlaweb.gob.ve/todochavez/2446-discurso-de-proclamacion-del-comandante-presidente-electo-hugo-chavez-por-el-consejo-nacional-electoral

Donald Trump: 'I Am Your Voice' (2016, July 21). *CBS New York.* https://newyork.cbslocal.com/2016/07/21/donald-trump-speech-rnc/

Donald Trump Speech "Save America" Rally Transcript January 6. (2021, January 6). *Rev.* https://www.rev.com/blog/transcripts/donald-trump-speech-save-america-rally-transcript-january-6

Fallece el cardenal venezolano Rosalio Castillo Lara, crítico con el Gobierno de Chávez (2007, October, 16). *Europapress.* https://www.europapress.es/internacional/noticia-venezuela-fallece-cardenal-venezolano-rosalio-castillo-lara-critico-gobierno-chavez-20071016185249.html

Febres-Cordero, M. M., & Márquez, B. (2006). A statistical approach to assess referendum results: The Venezuelan recall referendum 2004. *International Statistical Review, 74*(3), 379–389.

Fitzduff, M. (Ed.). (2017). *Why irrational politics appeals: Understanding the allure of Trump.* Praeger. ABC–CLIO.

Fox News. (2017, April 28). President trump reflects on his first 100 days. https://www.foxnews.com/transcript/president-trump-reflects-on-his-first-100-days

Freedom House. (2021, n.d.). *Freedom in the World 2021. United States.* https://freedomhouse.org/country/united-states/freedom-world/2021

Full text: 2017 Donald Trump inauguration speech transcript. (2017, January 10). *Politico.* https://www.politico.com/story/2017/01/full-text-donald-trump-inauguration-speech-transcript-233907

Full text: Trump's 2017 speech transcript. (2017, September, 19). *Politico.* https://www.politico.com/story/2017/09/19/trump-un-speech-2017-full-text-transcript-242879

Golshan, T. (2017, February 24). The White House just barred major media outlets from a press briefing. *Vox.* https://www.independent.co.uk/news/world/americas/us-politics/donald-trump-female-reporter-press-conference-weijia-jiang-kaitlan-collins-megyn-kelly-a9599031.html

Grynbaum, M. (2018, November 13). CNN sues Trump administration for barring Jim Acosta from White House. *The New York Times*. https://www.nytimes.com/2018/11/13/business/media/cnn-jim-acosta-trump-lawsuit.html

Here's the full text of Donald Trump's victory speech. (2016, November 9). *CNN*. https://edition.cnn.com/2016/11/09/politics/donald-trump-victory-speech/index.html

Higgins, A. (2017, February 26). Trump embraces 'Enemy of the People,' a phrase with a fraught history. *The New York Times*. ttps://www.nytimes.com/2017/02/26/world/europe/trump-enemy-of-the-people-stalin.html

Hugo Chávez amenaza con hacer desaparecer partidos. (2008, October 12). https://www.eluniverso.com/2008/10/12/0001/14/E97DEE0B3EF54BCCBDDA0E1BFCD07C42.html

Hugo Chavez's electoral reforms. (2009. August 7). *FairVote*. https://www.fairvote.org/hugo-chavezs-electoral-reforms

Human Rights Watch. (2002, July 2). *Political crisis in Venezuela*. https://www.hrw.org/legacy/backgrounder/americas/venezuela-bck0703.htm

Human Rights Watch. (2012). *Concentración y abuso de poder en la Venezuela Chávez.* https://www.hrw.org/es/report/2012/07/17/concentracion-y-abuso-de-poder-en-la-venezuela-de-chavez

Human Rights Watch. (2021, n.d.). *United States. Events of 2020.* https://www.hrw.org/world-report/2021/country-chapters/united-states

IACHR. (2003, n.d.). *Report on the situation of human rights in Venezuela.* http://www.cidh.org/countryrep/venezuela2003eng/intro.htm

Jamieson, K. H., & Taussig, D. (2017). Disruption, demonization, deliverance, and norm destruction: The rhetorical signature of Donald J. Trump. *Political Science Quarterly, 132*(4), 619–651.

Kopan, T. (2015, November, 29). 10 groups Donald Trump offended since launching his campaign. *CNN*. https://edition.cnn.com/2015/11/27/politics/donald-trump-insults-groups-list/index.html

Lakoff, G. [@George Lakoff]. (2017, February 20). *A Taxonomy of Trump's Tweets #protectthetruth* [Tweet]. Twitter. https://twitter.com/georgelakoff/status/833498095153344512?lang=en

Lardieri, A. (2019, July 2). One-third believe media are 'Enemy of the People'. *US News*. https://www.usnews.com/news/politics/articles/2019-07-02/poll-one-third-of-americans-believe-media-are-enemy-of-the-people

Lugo-Ocando, J., & Cañizález, A. (2021). The return of the caudillos in the digital age–changing hegemony and media caesarism: Continuities and changes in the news media landscape under the chavismo. In *When media succumbs to rising authoritarianism* (pp. 90–105). Routledge.

Maingon, T., & Welsch, F. (2009). Venezuela 2008: Hoja de ruta hacia el socialismo autoritario. *Revista de Ciencia Politica, 29*(2), 633–656. doi: 10.4067/S0718-090X2009000200018.

McCarthy, J. (2013, March 6). Loved or loathed, hugo chavez was the ultimate showman. *NPR*. https://www.npr.org/sections/thetwo-way/2013/03/06/173646204/remembering-hugo-chavez

McCarthy, N. (2021, January 11). End of the road for Trump's Twitter account. *Statista*. https://www.statista.com/chart/19561/total-number-of-tweets-from-donald-trump/

Mercieca, J. (2020, June 19). A field guide to Trump's dangerous rhetoric. *The Conversation*. https://theconversation.com/a-field-guide-to-trumps-dangerous-rhetoric-139531

Nelson, L., & Swanson, K. (2017, August 15). Full transcript: Donald Trump's press conference defending the Charlottesville rally. *Vox*. https://www.vox.com/2017/8/15/16154028/trump-press-conference-transcript-charlottesville

Nesbit, J. (2016, December 9). Donald Trump is the first true reality TV president. *Time*. https://time.com/4596770/donald-trump-reality-tv/

Norris, P., & Inglehart, R. (2019) *Cultural backlash: The rise of authoritarian-populism*. Cambridge University Press.

Phillips, A. (2018, October 3). 'You're not thinking. You never do,' Trump tells a female reporter. *The Washington Post*. https://www.washingtonpost.com/politics/2018/10/01/youre-not-thinking-you-never-do-trump-tells-female-reporter/

Pindell, J. (2020, July 2). Trump's 'Sleepy Joe' nickname for Biden isn't working. Even Trump knows it. *The Boston Globe*. https://www.bostonglobe.com/2020/07/02/metro/trumps-sleepy-joe-nickname-biden-isnt-working-even-trump-knows-it/

Quealy, K. (2021, January 19). The complete list of Trump's Twitter insults (2015-2021). *The New York Times*. https://www.nytimes.com/interactive/2021/01/19/upshot/trump-complete-insult-list.html

Römer Pieretti, M. (2014). Venezuela a partir de Chávez: Identidad cultural y política. *Historia y comunicación social*, *19*, 55–65.

Romero Rodríguez, L. M., & Römer Pieretti, M. (2016). Proceso de demonización de la oposición política en los hitos discursivos de Hugo Chávez según la prensa digital. *Temas de Comunicación*. (32), pp. 95–124. (2016). ISSN 2443-430.

Roose, K. (2021, June15). What is QAnon, the viral pro-Trump conspiracy theory? *The New York Times*. https://www.nytimes.com/article/what-is-qanon.html

Rosenberg, P. (2019, August 14). Trump dominates the media through Twitter: We knew this, but now there's science. *Salon*. https://www.salon.com/2019/08/04/trump-dominates-the-media-through-twitter-we-knew-this-but-now-theres-science/

Rubin, J. (2020, August 14). Opinion: Trump confesses to voter suppression. *The Washington Post*. https://www.washingtonpost.com/opinions/2020/08/13/trump-confesses-voter-supression/

Savage, C. (2020, April 14). Trump's claim of total authority in crisis is rejected across ideological lines. *The New York Times*. https://www.nytimes.com/2020/04/14/us/politics/trump-total-authority-claim.html

Sclafani, J. (2018). *Talking Donald Trump. A sociolinguistic study of style, meta-discourse, and political identity*. Routledge.

Sillito, D. (2016, November 14). Donald Trump: How the media created the president. *BBC News*. https://www.bbc.com/news/entertainment-arts-37952249

Stout, D. (2006, September 20). Chávez calls Bush 'the Devil' in U.N. speech. *The New York Times.* https://www.nytimes.com/2006/09/20/world/americas/20cnd-chavez.html

Suk, J. (2020, May 2). The Supreme Court confronts Trump's challenge to the separation of powers. *The New Yorker.* https://www.newyorker.com/news/our-columnists/the-supreme-court-confronts-trumps-challenge-to-the-separation-of-powers

The Apprentice. (n.d.). *TV Insider.* https://www.tvinsider.com/show/the-apprentice/

Tilley, C., Hoad, N., & Spraggo, B. (2017, December 13). Trumped: How Donald Trump dominates the news. *ABC News.* https://www.abc.net.au/news/2017-12-13/donald-trump-news-media-coverage/9125810?nw=0

Tribune Service News. (1999, February 3). President takes oath, blasts constitution. *Chicago Tribune.* https://www.chicagotribune.com/news/ct-xpm-1999-02-03-9902030256-story.html

Trump accuses Biden of being a 'socialist'. (2020, September 30). *The Independent.* [YouTube] [video file]. https://www.youtube.com/watch?v=W7JqTrBAELg

Trump, D. [@realDonaldTrump] (2017a, February 17). *The fake news media* [Tweet]. Twitter. https://twitter.com/home

Trump, D. [@realDonaldTrump]. (2017b, May 12). *Q1: Maybe the best thing* [Tweet]. Twitter. https://twitter.com/home

Trump, D., & Trump, D. [@realDonaldTrump]. (2017c, May 30). *The US Senate should switch.* [Tweet]. Twitter. https://twitter.com/home

Trump, D. [@realDonaldTrump]. (2017d, October 11). *Network news has become* [Tweet]. Twitter. https://twitter.com/home

Twitter, Inc. (2021, January 8). *Permanent suspension of @realDonaldTrump.* https://blog.twitter.com/en_us/topics/company/2020/suspension

Van Syckle, K. (2021, January 26). Five years, thousands of insults: Tracking Trump's invective. *The New York Times.* https://www.nytimes.com/2021/01/26/insider/Trump-twitter-insults-list.html

Vinogradoff, L. (2009, January 18). Chávez cierra las primeras 34 emisoras de radio y un canal de televisión. *ABC.* https://www.abc.es/internacional/abci-chavez-cierra-primeras-emisoras-radio-y-canal-telev Chávez's Aló Presidente and its impact on Venezuela's journalistic practice ision-200908010300-923015872249_noticia.html

Winberg, O. (2017). Insult politics: Donald Trump, right-wing populism, and incendiary language. *European Journal of American Studies, 12,* 12–2.

Wittmeyer, A. P. Q. (2013, March 13). The Bullyvarian Revolution: Hugo Chávez's most memorable insults. *Foreign Policy.* https://foreignpolicy.com/2013/03/06/the-bullyvarian-revolution-hugo-chavezs-most-memorable-insults/

Young, I. M. (1997). Difference as a resource for democratic communication. In J. Bohman & W. Rehg (Eds.), *Deliberative democracy: Essays on reason and politics* (pp. 383–404). MIT Press. https://ebookcentral-proquest-com.ezproxy.library.uq.edu.au/lib/uql/detail.action?docID=3338820#

6 The moral language of populist communication

In the sixth and final chapter, I discuss my main findings and identify some of the key indicators and implications of discursive disruption in Hugo Chávez's Venezuela and Donald Trump's US. I also attempt to answer this study's main research questions posed in Chapter 1, culminating with a reflection on the moral language of political communication and its links with the process or logic I have called discursive disruption.

I started the book by asking whether there is a connection between rising populist rhetoric and disrupted and weakening discourses of democracy. I also asked about the political communication strategies that would enable populist leaders to disrupt fostered discourses of modern democracy. I will start by answering the second question first. Across five chapters, I have examined the way the populist communicators Chávez and Trump have disrupted the discourses of democracy that predated their respective rise to power and through which they were elected. Through a Constitutional Assembly and riding the wave of his first presidential election popularity, Chávez initiated the change of the Venezuelan political system from representative to a so called "participative" democracy, which instead of being really participatory put all the power in the president's hands, and especially his *words*.

My second case study demonstrated how Donald Trump, mobilized and exacerbated resentments and alienation of ultra-conservative, white working-class Americans and irrational conspiracy theories attacking "liberal" Democrats (the so called "left" in the US), civil rights, and the Washington elite. Trump mobilized and incited his base to the point of insurrection just by maneuvering or playing with words. Trump also changed the attitude of the majority of the Republican Party toward democracy. Since Trump's presidential defeat, extreme right, openly racist, and progun Republican factions has been invested in subverting the 2020 elections, suppressing the vote of minority groups in various states, and obstructing most of Biden's policies. A

DOI: 10.4324/9781003118602-6

poll released by NGO Democracy Fund (Drutman, 2021), when I was finishing this manuscript, indicated that 86% of Republicans agreed that Trump's legal challenges were appropriate, and 68% believe that he really won the election. These results indicate the level of trust and legitimacy that Trump's base places on his Big Lie arguments. This is alarming in a country that has constructed itself as the global champion and moderator of democracy. But it also demonstrates the symbolic, emotional, irrational character of legitimacy, and trust.

Legitimacy in this case lies in the words of a charismatic populist leader, not on electoral results. It is a legitimacy that gives Trump, as it used to give Chávez, the power to incite others to coerce, subvert, and commit material acts of violence on the leader's name.

Both Chávez and Trump disrupted the discourses and conventions of democracy within democracy, which raises questions about whether democracy and those who believe in it can resist and correct the paths of disruptions born of democracy itself.

In this book I have studied discursive disruption, a process and a framework that defines and analyzes disruptions in the discourses of democracy, disruptions that I suggested as originally *discursive* and *communicative*, instigated by the persuasive, often insulting words of populist leaders like Chávez and Trump who governed as antipolitical outsiders and demonstrated their will to challenge the same laws that helped them be elected to office.

And, throughout these pages, I have showcased Chávez's and Trump's styles of populist communication, characterized by the use of four fundamental strategies: (1) antagonistic and insulting language that is irrational and intolerant against opponents; (2) a form of identity politics which, in both cases, exalt the virtues of the sovereign, patriotic peoples of their countries, a symbolic and exclusive construct that only considers likeminded, equally populist audiences, and excludes *the rest* (the opposed, the incompatible, or uncooperative), which I call the *nonpopulist,* an idea defined in the next section; (3) a savvy and confrontational use of all forms of media; and (4) a political communication style that bypasses or disrespects the discourses, values, norms of interaction, and principles of modern democracy. Through the operation of these four strategies, Chávez and Trump have disrupted democracy within democracy in their respective countries, installing what Palacio Martin (2017) called "a time of absolute democratic confusion" (para. 3).

6.1 The discursive ethos of populist power

One of the contributions of my analysis is defining the difference between populists and nonpopulists. I have suggested that populist leaders tend to bond with their loyal followers and alienate *the rest*, the *nonpopulist*. I define the nonpopulist as those individuals and groups who believe in democratic values and conventions and the possibility of civil, polite dialogue, and negotiations in plural environments, where they can listen to others without intending to change, dismiss or obliterate the other. As Sartori (1997) suggested, understanding pluralism entails "an understanding of tolerance, consensus, dissent, and conflict" (p. 64). For nonpopulists the aim is not totality, hatred or cancelation vis-à-vis the other, but *communication*, listening to each other. Nonpopulist individuals or groups would thrive in systems such as Young's (1997) communicative democracy, where plural dialogue between the different, devoid of insults or abuse, would flourish.

Another implication of my analysis is the confirmation of the *discursive ethos of populist power*. I define populist power as a communicative type of power that enables populist leaders to make others do their bidding on behalf of "the people", when, in reality, it works on behalf of the populist leader's own autocratic ends. Power that is disruptive as it mobilizes and incites audiences *through words*. Discursive power legitimizes the populist leader's discourses *emotionally* and *irrationally*. Leaders such as Chávez and Trump have exerted populist power to trigger controversy, prompting their constituents to do their will, all within and through democracy, but maiming democracy itself in the process. Chávez and Trump are *political jammers*, politicians who build power by breaking the discursive rules of the same system that enables them to perform.

The above discussion makes it possible now to answer my main research question. The three connecting themes or links between populist communication and disrupted discourses of democracy, are characterized by the predominance of, (a) authoritarian, intolerant, insulting language that is contrary to democratic values and civil coexistence; (b) extreme, polarizing, positions that implicitly or explicitly reduce plural and dialogic spaces that have *ideally* characterized the discourses of conventional or traditional democracy; and, (c) disruptive political environments where antidemocratic discourses reign. Seen together, these links make up the main indicators of discursive disruption. I will supply next some typical texts from my two case studies to illustrate these indicators.

a   Autocratic, divisive, and intolerant language

The first indicator of discursive disruption is the way the autocratic, divisive, insulting loyalty-seeking language of the two studied populist leaders (Chávez and Trump) dominated the political and media agenda in my two case studies. In a rally in 2010, commemorating the end of the last military dictatorship led by Marcos Perez Jiménez, which was toppled by united democratic groups in 1958, Chávez demanded something that paradoxically clashed with the values of pluralism and democracy, "absolute loyalty". Defiant and using swear words (*carajo*), he said,

> I demand absolute loyalty to my leadership! Because I am not me...I am a people, carajo!...I am not an individual...I am a people, and the people must be respected and I am under the obligation to secure that the people get that respect. The people I love and to whom I will give my whole life.... I demand loyalty. Anything else is treason.
>
> (Chávez, 2010)

At the beginning of Trump's government, in the midst of the stormy events that surrounded the creation of the Special Commission that investigated Russian interference in the 2016 elections, known popularly as the Muller Probe (Panetta, 2019), former FBI director James Comey said that the president told him at a private meeting "I need loyalty, I expect loyalty" (Taylor, 2017, para. 7).

Later in the year, the defeat of the Republican Party in the gubernatorial and municipal elections in the state of Virginia was interpreted by legacy media, especially *CNN*, as Trump's first loss (Cilliza, 2017); however, Trump tried to rewrite history by blaming losing candidate Ed Gillespie for not having sought his presidential endorsement. Trump tweeted:

> Ed Gillespie worked hard but did not embrace me or what I stand for. Don't forget, Republicans won 4 out of 4 House seats, and with the economy doing record numbers, we will continue to win, even bigger than before!.
>
> (Trump, 2017a)

Thus, with populist Trump or Chávez you are either with them or against them; and, in the case of Chávez, being against him or *the people* (terms that he used as if they were exchangeable) is treason. Both Chávez and Trump have been deemed as inciters of violence, who with their words and antidialogic discourse became the "accelerant" (Cineas, 2021) of disruptions and in some cases material violence by loyal groups. Chávez incited and disrupted through his "Bolivarian Circles" and also the armed "Bolivarian militia", a vertical structure that distorted the role and structure of the Venezuelan armed forces. These armed militia could be mobilized by Chávez directly and at whim (as it was not regulated by the constitution or any laws) against not only international but especially local political opponents ("Chávez Fortalece", 2011).

Trump incited his extreme loyalist groups (QAnon, Oath Keeper, Proud Boys, and others) to the 6 January Capitol insurrection. The way he steered them to the Capitol was so obvious in his speech that it was the main allegation used by the House of Representatives for his second impeachment. At his "Save America" rally in Washington, on January 6 2021, Trump invited members of these groups attending his rally to "fight like hell" to "stop the steal" of the 2020 election. He said, "Something's wrong here. Something is really wrong. Can't have happened. And we fight. We fight like Hell and if you don't fight like Hell, you're not going to have a country anymore" ("Donald Trump Speech", 2021, para. 78).

Incitation by words was the way Chávez and Trump helped to disrupt their respective polities through boosting their antipolitical, antidialogic and antagonistic ideologies and actions, the delegitimization of democracy, and the obstruction, shrinkage or eventual disappearance of spaces for political dialogue.

b   Chávez's and Trump's roles in the shrinkage of shared spaces for dialogue

The second indicator of discursive disruption lies in the shrinkage, blockage and even disappearance of pluralistic spaces for dialogue. Chávez's and Trump's intolerant postures and thirst for loyalty and total power unavoidably led both presidents to promote radical or extreme positions. Dialogue between plural actors became difficult or impossible during, and even after they left office. Their respective proxies and loyalists have guaranteed that the permanent controversy feeding Chavismo or Trumpism remains.

Chávez's Venezuela has been marked by the impossibility of dialogue or compromise between chavistas and antichavistas. There were some dialogue initiatives, especially in Chávez's weakest or unpopular moments, in 2002 and 2003, a propos the coup and oil strike that aimed to topple him; the dialogue was mainly initiated and led by the Organization of American States (OAS) and the Carter Center. Overall, these negotiations between Chávez and his representatives, and the members of the *"Coordinadora Democratica"*, an ad hoc group formed by different (and often at odds with each other) opposition groups lasted too long to the benefit of Chávez (who became stronger as time passed), and the detriment of an exhausted and divided opposition and the distrust of equally exhausted divided, demoralized citizens. Anomie, understood as the loss of ethical democratic codes, reigned. It was a symbolic diplomatic gesture by the international initiators with no genuine interest or commitment on the part of Chávez or his opponents to compromise or reach consent (see McCoy & Diez, 2011; also, Sanchez Melean, 2005); a public show that complied with facilitators and public opinion. The lack of results increased citizens' distrust and delegitimization of any conversation or electoral process that would follow.

In 2004, Chávez won the Recall Referendum by a narrow margin, in questioned results. Chávez also won the 2006 Presidential elections and in 2007, attempted to change the constitution again to make Venezuela a socialist country in a referendum that he lost, his first loss in nearly a decade in power. So, 2007 marked a year of rage and vindictiveness when Chávez repeatedly threatened the opposition. In 2009, after winning a constitutional referendum that made it possible for him to be re-elected indefinitely, he felt so empowered at that moment that he proclaimed that any type of dialogue similar to those that were held to reach pacts between party leaders were "over" (Europa Press, 2009), adding that anyone who wanted dialogue could have it every day but "with the people" (para. 2), that is, *with him,* a symbolic claim that really meant that there was no possibility of dialogue. Government and opposition spoke different languages in what became a Babelian reality. The opposition have abstained from participation in several electoral processes since 2005. In 2007, Chávez launched his ultimate threat, again using *the people* as a shield or excuse: Voters must be *with* him (and *the people*), or against him, which now not only meant treason but death. This happened in his speech commemorating the defeat of the coup attempted by some opposing groups in 2002; his words show a bitter revenge, antidialogic tone:

> ... Here we say: Patria, socialism or death!...Either we are, or we are not, the Bible says: "You cannot serve two masters at the same time", "You cannot be right with God and with the Devil at the same time", or you are right with God or you are right with the Devil, choose, we have chosen.
>
> (Conmemoración del quinto, 2007, para. 129).

The cry "Patria, Socialism or death", which became a mandatory salute in the Venezuelan armed forces, embodied the completion of Chávez's communicative hegemony, that is, final closure, political communication shutdown. A situation, which, at least in 21st century Venezuela, has led to an increase of disenfranchisement, uncertain or anxious public moods, distrust in democratic processes, and generalized political exhaustion, while Chávez's successor, Maduro, has remained in power.

Donald Trump's critical discourses (a) against Obamacare and gun control; (b) in favor of travel bans and regulating immigration and ending the US's participation in the G20 and the Paris carbon emissions agreements; and (c) his controversial statements about the way the Constitution limited his presidential power, also marked extreme positions with no possibility for compromise. His defiant and abusive language against protesters was mimicked by ultraconservative sheriffs of police (such as former controversial Sherriff Joe Arpaio) who used Trump's politically incorrect language and "more controversial, pro-incarceration views than in recent years", alarming legal observers who fear an "increasingly undisciplined justice system" (Craig, 2017, para. 7).

Jennifer Mercieca (2020) explained, "Trump campaigned as an unaccountable leader. He promised that he would fight for his followers and wouldn't be accountable to established leaders in his party, the media, fact-checkers, political correctness, or common standards of decency" (para. 7). Antipluralism, intolerance, and impoliteness were replicated in Chávez's and Trump's foreign policy discourses; a recent and rare study on both leaders' international performances by Thiers and Wehner (2021), suggested a predominance of "noncooperative and conflict-inducing behavior in the international arena" (p. 1).

The "Save America" speech in January 2021 (cited in Chapter 5) was a typical illustration of Trump's antidialogic character. He said then that he will "never concede", the same attitude that he had had throughout his government (see "Donald Trump Speech", 2021).

Professor Gayle Allard (2020) suggested that doing politics in a deeply divided country will not be easy in the US. The two extreme groups at play have "radically different" worldviews. Allard (2020) explained that on the "far right side" (para. 3) emerged a new or revamped group, formed mainly by little educated white inhabitants of rural areas, that defend the right to own guns, reject abortion, and globalization. On the other side, a group formed by urban, diverse, younger, and more educated Americans emerged. This group, loosely and often pejoratively called liberal or "woke" promote the protection of the environment, social justice, "and embrace a more diverse, multicultural society." (para. 3).

Although the US has been divided by ideology, values, race, and geography from the beginning of its existence as a nation, Trump, like Chávez, peddled on identity differences exacerbating existing divisions. They have nurtured conflict and antagonism. Dialogue would weaken them, make them fade.

c   Increasing unrest, protests, physical, and discursive violence and disruption

Finally, the third indicator, points to transgressions, erosion, and changes in the discourses and conventions of democracy. The analysis showed that in their own ways, in their own contexts, cultures and times, Chávez's and Trump's authoritarian, intolerant language, identity politics, savvy and controversial use of the media, and disparaging attitude vis-à-vis democratic discourses and conventions triggered events that have had a disruptive impact on their respective polities.

In Hugo Chávez's Venezuela, and throughout his 13-year government, there was an escalation of protests, polarization, division, and outrage. The watchdog organization Venezuelan Observatory of Violence published a report, authored by Pimentel and González (2020) that documented 100 thousand protests between 2000 and 2020, all of which defended political and economic freedoms, civil rights, and protested against specific acts of coercion and violence, basic goods shortages, workers unions rights, increasing decay in public services (water, power), and the general malaise that has prevailed in Venezuelan during the Chávez era. Venezuela has lived through two decades of permanent social conflict and economic decay; pluralist party democracy was erased as Chávez preferred to ally with autocrats, international terrorists, and narcotraffic capos than with opposition politicians in his own country.

Weakening separation of power and electoral transparency have also been documented by the UN, OAS, international institutions, and NGOs since 2006, when Chávez radicalized his language and political stance (see Human Rights Watch, 2008; 2012). In 2005, the opposition decided not to participate in the parliamentary elections alleging lack of electoral transparency; hence, only Chávez's candidates were elected. The end of separation of powers was consummated. These events also demonstrate that democracy is not only about elections. Despite at least 26 electoral processes during the Chávez era, all the other indicators of democracy (separation of power, rule of law, independence of the judiciary, respect for freedoms, and civil rights, etc.) have been trampled everyday by the chavista regime.

With only 4 years in power, Trump's discursive disruption process could be evaluated not only through the number of protests, riots and the 6th January insurrection, but also by the messy way he misinterpreted democracy and used verbal violence to jam politics.

Between 2015 and 2017 there was an increase of protests, riots, and rallies against and pro Trump in major cities of the US. The extreme right groups (QAnon, Proud Boys, Oath Keepers, and others) and extreme left (anti-fascist and anti-racist Antifa) have been more active and violent during Trump's presidency. Both in his rallies and TV appearances, Trump inflamed his base through cue words such as the memorable '"Proud Boys, stand back and stand by! But I'll tell you what, somebody's got to do something about Antifa and the left"' (Smith et al., 2020, para 3). Thus, the first two years of Trump's presidency were especially convulsive. Similar to Chavez, Trump tried to ensure the implementation of some of his promises (the Mexico–US wall, travel bans, scrapping Obamacare, etc.) taking advantage of his initial popularity. The 2016 primaries, presidential election, and inauguration were prolific with protests that increased on an almost daily basis. During this period, cities like Washington, Berkley, Charlottesville, Boston, and Portland saw significant violence and confrontation. Chenoweth and Pressman (2017) reported that by September 2017 there had been 578 protests, demonstrations, strikes, marches, sit-ins, and rallies in the US, at least one in every state and district, with a participation of between 80,130 and 89,854 people. Opposition against Trump's discourse and policies drove 85.1% of the events. "About 68.7 percent overall were explicitly anti-Trump while another 16.4 percent overall took stances on issues that contradict the president" (Chenoweth & Pressman, 2017, para. 5), on issues like advocating for workers' rights or protesting pipelines, the end of the Deferred Action for Childhood Arrivals (DACA) program, racism, and police shootings.

Fisher et al. (2019) also researched the number and type of mobilizations against Trump in the period 2016–2019, which, they argued, were a demonstration of citizens' concern and rejection of Trump's discourses and policies in times of extreme polarization. Fisher et al. (2019, p. 1) indicated,

> Millions of Americans have marched and rallied in a number of massive, multilocation protests, including the Women's March (2017, 2018, and 2019), the March for Science (2017, 2018, and 2019), the March for Our Lives (2018), Families Belong Together (2018), the National Student Walkout (2018), and the Global Climate Strikes (2019).

Trump's presidency saw the longest government shutdown in American history, 35 days of blocked political dialogue all over his wish (or rather calculated whim) to build a wall with Mexico to stop Mexican and other Latin American immigrants (or "bad hombres" as he used to call them), a proposal that was cheered by his patriotic fans. The shutdown ended after he had to relent on the wall (Restuccia et al., 2019), although after he continued pushing for it during his 2020 campaign.

Trump's lack of understanding of separation of powers, rule of law, and the constitution in general was especially reflected in one his tweets questioning a judge's authority on his controversial travel bans. On February 4, 2017, Trump tweeted,

> What is our country coming to when a judge can halt a Homeland Security Protests, and anyone, even with bad intentions, can come into U.S.
>
> (Trump, 2017b).

About the same topic, the BBC News reproduced a statement by Democratic Senator Patrick Leahy, from the Senate judiciary committee, who said, "The President's hostility toward the rule of law is not just embarrassing, it is dangerous... He seems intent on precipitating a constitutional crisis" (2017, para. 11–12).

With just 4 years in power, Trump both challenged and disrupted institutional conventions, rituals, and protocols in the management of the Executive, Congress, his own party, FBI, diplomacy electoral rules, and relations with the media. After their 2018 summit in Helsinki, Trump even sided with Putin against the FBI when Putin said that Russia had not meddled in the 2016 elections: "President Putin says it's not Russia. I don't see any reason why it would be" ("Trump Sides", 2018, para. 6). Statements like this are a concern considering that a study by The Pew Research Center indicated that 40% of Trump's followers get their information solely from *Fox News* (see Gottfried et al., 2017).

In sum, my analysis thus far confirms a trend: Chávez's and Trump's speech performances are deeply intertwined with episodes of disruption in their respective polities. After nearly 20 years of chavista discourse, Venezuela is a dramatically divided country, where daily anti-government (verbal and physical) protests, generalized unrest and anxiety, and humanitarian and financial crisis, are blatantly dismissed by the small group that rules the country by mimicking the late president's language and ways. This state of permanent conflict has closed many possibilities of dialogue, mutual recognition, or democratic coexistence.

The three indicators of discursive disruption that I have showcased here, namely, (a) authoritarian, autocratic, loyalty-demanding language, (b) shrinkage of shared spaces for dialogue, and

(c) disruptions in the discourses and conventions of democracy expressed in increasing protests and generalized unrest, ultimately suggest that there is something wrong in democracy, that the system is not functioning, and that the political disenchantment expressed by some groups should not be neglected as marginal or as not being "us", or part of "who we are". Rather, the disenchantments of these groups, usually populist audiences, may provide some clues for possible solutions to disruptive political environments. Clues that point to work hard on refining, rebuilding, or changing the way our democratic discourses represent cultural diversity and the urgent need of more plural, civil, and inclusive discussion of ideas. These clues also point to ethical discussions of how political and media players and increasingly engaged citizens should live their lives together in the community, recognizing and listening to each other instead of exacerbating their differences. Figure 6.1 graphically represents the indicators and implications of discursive disruption.

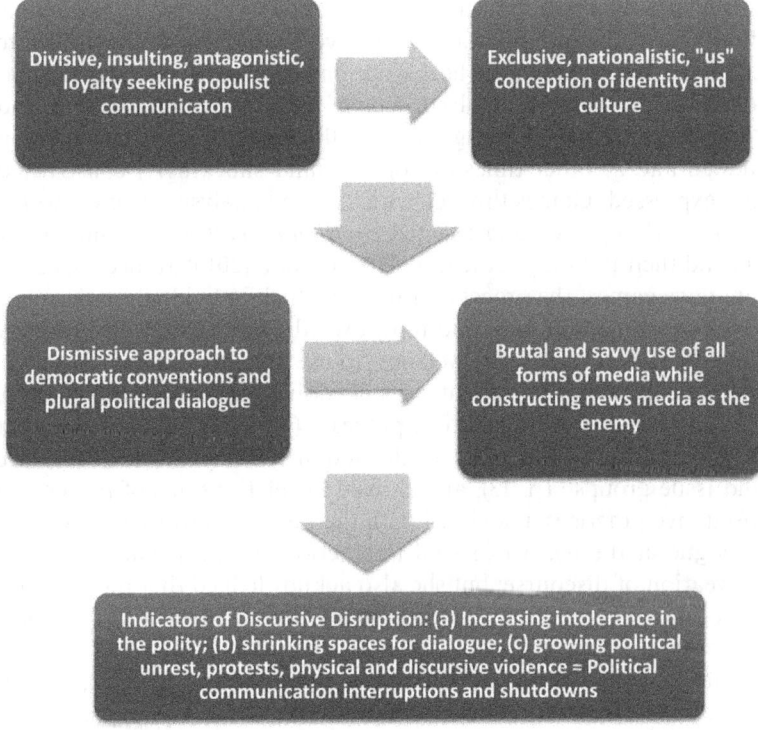

Figure 6.1 Discursive Disruption Indicators and Implications Frame

The discussions about the indicators and implications of discursive disruption lead now to a final reflection on the moral language of populist communication.

6.2 The moral language of political communication, Chávez and Trump

As Ball et al. (1989) suggested, although language is the common tie that holds community together, it can become "worn and frayed" (p. 1), that is, shattered, violated, disrupted. The political conversation has been in some events, situations and even in whole countries, such as Chávez's Venezuela, temporarily or permanently interrupted and in some cases abused, violated. After all, as I suggested in previous chapters, populist communication is violence perpetrated against the language of plural democracy. Although I am not an ethicist and very far from being a moralist, at the heart of my study there is concern about the moral language of politics, and especially of populist communication and the disruptions it causes for and within democracy and its discourses. The populist talk, as I have been trying to demonstrate chapter after chapter, and the disruption processes it boosts in the dialogue within the polis involve a type of morality, moral nuances, and "language games", as Wittgenstein (2010) called them, that are often hidden and at other times are openly (and shockingly) constructed and expressed. Games through which, as my analysis suggests, words are *named*, repeated and enacted *confrontationally* by populist leaders and their populist audiences. Wittgenstein (2010) argued that such language games, the processes through which individuals and groups imagine, name, interpret and repeat words, are part of our everyday life. Populist players know well how to use language games.

Political discourse is about ways of "doing politics", which involves "all participants in the political process" (Van Dijk, 1997, p. 13), that is, politicians, citizens, news media, and their audiences and "pressure and issue groups" (p. 13), all involved in relationships of power and discursive practices associated with the polity. Bolivar (2018) located dialogue at the heart of social interactions between humans in the cocreation of discourse; but she also acknowledged that the presence of conflict, antagonism, and rupture are also at the heart of political discourses.

The concept of discursive disruption proposed by this book, encompasses both a concern and a critique about the way populist players weaponize antidialogic communication strategies and language expertly transmitted through all forms of media. The populist talk, specifically, embodies an antagonistic type of ethics about how political life should be lived and approached in everyday experiences and interactions; it consists of language games that thrive on permanent confrontation and imaginaries of patriotism and identity (peculiar to each country) to demonize and exclude opponents (the nonpopulist), and to include, connect, and bond with the likeminded. The populist talk and the discursive disruption it entails (that eventually manages not only to jam, maim, and even change the discourses and conventions of democracy) decries dialogue, negotiation, and consensus, in the construction of populist power and identity.

Ball et al. (1989) argued that a moral political language should be viewed as "a medium of shared understanding and an arena of action because the concepts embedded in it inform the belief and practices of political agents" (p. 1). In the case of democracy, a moral language is the language that promotes the defense of freedoms; social justice, civil rights; rule of law, separation of power, and plural and rational deliberation. Arguably, the main types of democracy in the literature (liberal, representative, deliberative, discursive, and communicative) share in different proportions some or all the aforementioned values and principles.

Interpretations about the moral language of politics are closely associated with discussions in the literature about politeness, civility, and incivility (see Álvarez, 2009; Álvarez & Chumaceiro, 2011; Herbst, 2010; Kaul de Marlangeon, 2008; Kaul de Marlangeon & Cordisco, 2014). Susan Herbst (2010), in her book called *Rude Democracy*, explained how incivility has been traditionally used by Republicans in the US as a "strategic weapon" to trigger emotions, disrupt discussions, or meetings and get the attention of legacy media and social media conversations. Discussions, for example, about Obamacare turned so volatile and angry that Republicans achieved a double aim: controlled the agenda and stopped, and even shutdown, the discussion on the topic. Venezuelan discourse scholars Álvarez and Chumaceiro (2011) studied deliberate insults and impoliteness toward the adversary as a way to promote "emotional adhesion to followers" (p. 137). And in their study of the discourses used in Argentinian politics, Kaul de Marlangeon and Cordisco (2014) argued that verbal impoliteness has seen a rebirth and revamping in social media environments, especially in Facebook and Twitter; they suggested that the strategic use of online impoliteness exacerbates impolite behavior among social media users, naturalizing its use in social networks.

Thus, populism (of all signs, right or left) embodies *a type of moral language or discourse* that thrives on confrontation and disruption, demonization of the "enemy" (usually represented by the establishment and legacy media), and the glorification of the unsatisfied or "forgotten" *people*. Instead of a vehicle of "shared understanding" (Ball et al., 1989), or "redemption", as Adorno (2005) envisioned it in his *Minima Moralia*, the antidialogic and antagonistic language used by populist leaders has become a medium of shared conflict, coercion, and communicative violence. My study has analized how in the voices of populist players like Chávez and Trump, dialectic redemption and democratic dialogue can indeed turn into coercion, discursive violence, and communicative closure.

Political communication scholar Silvio Waisbord (2018) proposed the idea of a "communication commons", consisting of democratic spaces for "diversity, tolerance, reasons, and fact" (p. 21), where citizens agree or disagree about political issues in pluralistic contexts, where dialogue and not confrontation reigns. This concept is consistent with Young's (1996) "communicative democracy", with the idea of building environments that facilitate plural political dialogue so that together we seek solutions for collective problems in our respective polities. The disruptive rhetoric used by populist leaders such as Chávez and Trump, not only contradicts the idea of a communication commons or communicative democracy but rather seeks the moral invalidation and exclusion of their opponents.

The limitations of studying these two populist characters together have been mainly located in their completely different cultural, political, social, and ideological backgrounds. However, as de la Torre (2016) argued, both Chávez and Trump have been characterized as "populist autocrats" that communicate and act from within the system that elected them, "strangling" democracy "by attacking civil liberties, regulating the public sphere and using the legal system to silence critics. Americans who value an inclusive, tolerant and pluralist country need to be on guard against Mr. Trump's following in their footsteps" (para. 13).

Throughout the analysis I have critically showcased the communicative and media dimensions of populism and documented how populist leaders tend to lead conflictive relationships with the media to communicate and dominate the agenda. They call the media the enemy, which has become an idiosyncratic trait of their respective communicative styles. Both, Chávez and Trump, in their own context and times, took advantage of media outlets and platforms driven by emotional trends, hashtags, clickbait, influencers, and widespread management of their likeminded audiences (the sovereign patriotic people in their case). Both leaders have been cunning manipulators of media power and populist power to foment a sense of direct communication with their constituents (avoiding the intermediation of journalism and institutions of democracy); and transmit feelings of individual/ collective empowerment to confront the enemy, their opponents, the nonpopulists, in the construction and management of their power.

Not dissimilar, at least in style, in the type of participatory media, to the way various Latin American populists used the media of their time (mainly films, radio, and newspapers) to construct power and nation (Fraiman, 2009). Latin American populists from the 1940s and 1950s (Peron in Argentina, Getulio Vargas in Brazil, and Lazaro Cárdenas in México) used film, radio, and soap operas to construct national identities and nationalistic imaginaries while controlling and censoring some of the main opposing media outlets of the time (Fraiman, 2009). Contemporary authoritarian populists, such as Chávez and Trump, not only have used all types of media to connect directly with their publics but also to issue policy, bully journalists and politicians, and criticize or even fire their staff. It could be argued that both Chávez and Trump have confronted the media *by expertly handling the same media.*

Both populist actors were elected in democratic elections within the rules of the political systems existing in their respective countries. However, once in power both attempted to change or skew some of the conventions of such systems.

CNN commentator Mel Robbins (2015) argued that to understand Donald Trump, one has to understand that,

> ... he's "the disrupter." The disrupter is someone whose entire "brand" is to break the mold, to turn the way we do things on its head. Amazon did this with retail, Uber did it with taxi services, Airbnb did it with travel, Tinder did it with dating, Slack is doing it with email, Spotify is doing it with music, peer-to-peer lending is changing banking. And Trump is disrupting politics.
>
> (para. 2–3).

Moreover, my analysis makes more urgent the concern of Bolivar (2018) about the use of insults and impoliteness to disrupt politics and democracy. She explained how in Chávez's Venezuela,

> the practice of insulting the 'enemies', initiated by a President in office, became institutionalized, spread to the whole population and filled the political scenario with hostility, anger, disrespect for the other, and eventually intensified the polarization process and nondialogical political culture.
>
> (p. 107)

Jack Cassidy's (2017) bleak analysis about Trump's Presidency being a "stress test" for American democracy and its values, should serve as a warning; he argues that practically every day Trump's narratives were aimed to undermine the values of democracy "spewing forth a never-ending torrent of divisiveness and venom." (para. 2); Cassidy's piece concluded with a warning:

> ...People who have witnessed other democracies fray and other divided countries come apart are looking on in dismay. Despite his promise to "Make America Great Again," Trump has delivered practically nothing except chaos, bombast, and division...
>
> (para. 11)

My critical study has documented and analyzed some of the ways in which Chávez's and Trump's used and abused of certain political communication strategies, namely, (1) intolerant, loyalty-demanding, violent and antagonistic rhetoric; (2) patriotic and exclusive construction of identity; (3) brutal and controversial yet savvy use of media; and (4) disrespect for the discourses, values, and conventions of democracy. Such communicative strategies have led to the situations of *discursive disruption* that have suffused their respective polities. Disruptive situations that can be recognized through three indicators, (a) ongoing confrontational discourses, (b) shrinking or nonexistent shared spaces for plural dialogue, and (c) generalized unrest and political confusion.

After nearly 20 years of chavista discourse, Venezuela is today a broken country where daily anti-government (verbal and physical) protests, unrest and anxiety, and humanitarian and financial crises are blatantly neglected and even manipulated by the small chavista group that rules the country by mimicking the late president's language and ways. The state of permanent conflict has closed possibilities of dialogue, mutual recognition, or democratic coexistence between the chavistas and opponents. In 2021, Norway facilitated talks between the factions for the second time (Rendon & Fernandez, 2021). However, after 21 years of chavismo, and the lack of commitment to dialogue, consent, and compromise by chavistas and opponents, Rendon and Fernandez (2021) have suggested, "this decision is likely to splinter political actors" (p. 8). Trust was lost in Venezuela throughout the Chávez era to the benefit of the chavistas in power. Anomie reigns in the Venezuelan polity.

With just 4 years in power, Trump has challenged and disrupted institutional conventions, rituals, and protocols in the management of the Executive, Congress, his own party, the FBI, the way to conduct diplomacy, electoral rules pushing vote suppression, and relations with the media. Since he rose to power there has been an intensification of violent protests and riots throughout the US, which have also been taken up in other countries. At the time of finishing this book, Trump was re-energizing his political power, building a multimillion-dollar platform media scaffold, with fundraising and digital political communication purposes (Silverman, 2021). At a rally in Iowa defiantly signaling his intention for 2024 candidacy and suggesting, tongue in cheek, that his slogan will be to "make America great again, again" (Zitser, 2021, para. 4). In the meantime, Joe Biden's ambitious post-Covid welfare agenda has been repeatedly stifled by a Congress deeply divided by the adversarial discourses and power ambitions of the extreme factions that flourished during the Trump years.

This critical and rather preliminary study has attempted to explore, document, define and critique disruptive communicative events in two countries where populist leaders have been in power. This book is an invitation to political communication scholars to inquire further about the disruptions encroached by populist leaders (like Chávez and Trump) upon the discourses of democracy, the process and frame that I have called *discursive disruption*.

References

Adorno, T. (2005). *Minima moralia: Reflections from damaged life*. Verso.
Allard, G. (2020, November 5). Finding common ground in a divided America. *Insights. Knowledge Driven Content*. https://www.ie.edu/insights/articles/finding-common-ground-in-a-divided-america/
Álvarez, A. (2009). Anticortesía y política. *Lengua y Habla*, (13), 19–33.
Álvarez, A., & Chumaceiro, I. (2011). Insulto e intolerancia: La confrontación en el macro diálogo político. *Preconceito e intolerância: re exões linguístico-discursivas*, 137–176.
Arendt, H. (1998). *The human condition*. The University of Chicago Press.
Ball, T., Farr, J., & Hanson, R. (1989). *Political innovation and conceptual change*. Cambridge University Press.
BBC News. (2017, February 6). Taking on Trump: Is the US facing a constitutional crisis? *BBC*. https://www.bbc.com/news/world-us-canada-38881119
Bolívar, A. (2018). *Political discourse as dialogue*. A Latin American perspective. Routledge.
Cassidy, J. (2017, October 16). Stress-Testing American Democracy· Nine Months of President Trump. *The New Yorker*. https://www.newyorker.com/news/john-cassidy/grading-donald-trumps-first-nine-months-in-office
Cilliza, C. (2017, November 8). Donald Trump was the big loser in Virginia. *CNN*. https://edition.cnn.com/2017/11/07/politics/northam-trump-virginia/index.html
Cineas, F. (2021, January 9). Donald Trump is the accelerant. *Vox*. https://www.vox.com/2150602d/trump-violence-tweets-racist-hate-speech

Chávez fortalece a las milicias bolivarianas. (2011, March 30). *El Tiempo*. https://www.eltiempo.com/archivo/documento/MAM-4475447

Chávez, H. (2010, February 1). Hugo Chávez: I demand absolute loyalty to my leadership. [Video]. YouTube. http://www.youtube.com/watch?v= swBsxRWAmbk

Chenoweth, E., & Pressman, J. (2017, November 1). Sometimes a handful of protesters can spark an enormous discussion. That certainly happened in September. *The Washington Post*. https://www.washingtonpost.com/news/ monkey-cage/wp/2017/11/01/sometimes-a-handful-of-protesters-can-spark-an-enormous-discussion-that-certainly-happened-in-september/

Conmemoración del quinto aniversario de los sucesos del 11 de abril de 2002. (2007, April 11). *Todo Chávez*. http://www.todochavez.gob.ve/todochavez/ 2574-conmemoracion-del-%20quinto-aniversario-de-los-sucesos-del-11-de-abril-de-2002

Craig, T. (2017, November 12). Tough-talking sheriffs raise their voices in Trump era. *The Washington Post*. https://www.washingtonpost.com/national/ tough-talking-sheriffs-raise-their-voices-in-trump-era/2017/11/12/98832d36-c04f-11e7-959c-fe2b598d8c00_story.html

de la Torre, C. (2016, December 15). Will democracy survive Trump's populism? Latin America may tell us. *The New York Times*. https://www.nytimes. com/2016/12/15/opinion/will-democracy-survive-trumps-populism-latin-america-may-tell-us.html

Donald Trump speech "Save America" rally transcript January 6. (2021, January 6). *Rev*. https://www.rev.com/blog/transcripts/donald-trump-speech-save-america-rally-transcript-january-6

Drutman, L. (2021, June n.d.). Theft perception. *Democracy Fund. Voters Study Group*. https://www.voterstudygroup.org/topic/elections

Europa Press. (2009, February 20). Chávez advierte de que 'se acabó' el diálogo con la oposición porque ya fue 'derrotada'. *Atlántico*. https://www. atlantico.net/articulo/mundo/chavez-advierte-acabo-dialogo-oposicion-porque-fue-derrotada/20090221194405057021.html

Fisher, D. R., Andrews, K. T., Caren, N., Chenoweth, E., Heaney, M. T., Leung, T., Perkins, L. N., & Pressman, J. (2019). The science of contemporary street protest: New efforts in the United States. *Science advances*, 5(10), eaaw5461.

Fraiman, J. A. (2009). Medios de comunicación masiva y populismo en América Latina: Posibles articulaciones para analizar los casos en el peronismo argentino, el getulismo brasileño y el cardenismo mexicano. *Razón y palabra*, 14(70), 1–34.

Gottfried, J., Barthel, M., & Mitchell, A. (2017, January 18). Trump, Clinton voters divided in their main source for election news. *Pew Research Center*. https://www.journalism.org/2017/01/18/trump-clinton-voters-divided-in-their-main-source-for-election-news/

Herbst, S. (2010). *Rude democracy: Civility and incivility in American politics*. Temple University Press.

Human Rights Watch. (2008). *A decade under Chávez: Political intolerance and lost opportunities for advancing human rights in Venezuela*. https://www.hrw. org/sites/default/files/reports/venezuela0908web.pdf

Human Rights Watch. (2012, July 17). *Tightening the grip: Concentration and abuse of power in Chávez's Venezuela.* https://www.hrw.org/report/2012/07/17/tightening-grip/concentration-and-abuse-power-chavezs-venezuela

Kaul de Marlangeon, S. (2008). Impoliteness in institutional and non-institutional contexts. *Pragmatics, 18*(4), 729–749.

Kaul de Marlangeon, S., & Cordisco, A. (2014). La descortesía verbal en el contexto político-ideológico de las redes sociales. *Revista de Filología,* 32, pp. 145–162. https://riull.ull.es/xmlui/handle/915/4645

McCoy, J., & Diez, F. (2011). *International mediation in Venezuela.* US Institute of Peace Press.

Mercieca, J. (2020, June 19). A field guide to Trump's dangerous rhetoric. *The Conversation.* https://theconversation.com/a-field-guide-to-trumps-dangerous-rhetoric-139531

Palacio Martin, J. (2017, October 23). El tiempo de la confusion democratica. *El Pais.* https://elpais.com/elpais/2017/10/20/opinion/1508513890_107029.html

Panetta, G. (2019, January 24). Here's how a grand jury works and why the government shutdown is affecting the grand juries in the Mueller investigation. *Business Insider.* https://www.businessinsider.com.au/how-mueller-grand-juries-work-mueller-investigation-government-shutdown-2019-1?r=US&IR=T

Pimentel, O., & González, A. (2020, August 28). Dos décadas de protestas en Venezuela. *Observatorio Venezolano de Violencia.* https://observatoriodeviolencia.org.ve/news/dos-decadas-de-protestas-en-venezuela/

Rendon, M., & Fernandez, C. (2021, May 24.). Lesson for negotiations in Venezuela: A Roadmap. *Centre for Strategic and International Studies.* https://www.csis.org/analysis/lessons-negotiations-venezuela-roadmap

Restuccia, A., Everett, B., & Caygle, H. (2019, January 25). Longest shutdown in history ends after Trump relents on wall. *Politico.* https://www.politico.com/story/2019/01/25/trump-shutdown-announcement-1125529

Robbins, M. (2015, June 16). Why Trump is beating Fox News – and GOP rivals. *CNN.* https://edition.cnn.com/2016/01/27/opinions/donald-trump-republican-robbins/index.html

Sanchez Melean, J. (2005). *The role of the OAS in the political crisis of Venezuela (April 11, 2002- May 31, 2003)* (Doctoral dissertation, Ohio University).

Sartori, G. (1997). Understanding pluralism. *Journal of Democracy, 8*(4), 58–69. http://dx.doi:10.1353/jod.1997.0064

Silverman, G. (2021, October 30). Why a Spac deal serves Trump's purposes. *Financial Times.* https://amp.ft.com/content/043b6015-9b0c-4bb1-9a95-6c1c99c26245#

Smith, D., Beckett, L., Singh, M., & Wong, J. C. (2020, September 30). Donald Trump refuses to condemn white supremacists at presidential debate. *The Guardian.* https://www.theguardian.com/us-news/2020/sep/29/trump-proud-boys-debate-president-refuses-condemn-white-supremacists

Taylor, J. (2017, June 7). Comey: Trump asked for 'Loyalty,' wanted him to 'Let' Flynn investigation 'Go'. *NPR.* https://www.npr.org/2017/06/07/531927032/comey-trump-asked-for-loyalty-wanted-him-to-let-flynn-investigation-go

Thiers, C., & Wehner, L. E. (2021). The personality traits of populist leaders and their foreign policies: Hugo Chávez and Donald Trump. *International Studies Quarterly*.

Trump, D. (2017b, February 4). [@realDonaldTrump]. *What is our country coming to*. [Tweet]. Twitter. https://twitter.com/home

Trump, D. (2017a, November 8). [@realDonaldTrump]. *Ed Gillespie worked hard but did not embrace me* [Tweet]. Twitter. https://twitter.com/home

Trump sides with Russia against FBI at Helsinki Summit. (2018, July 16). *BBC News*. https://www.bbc.com/news/world-europe-44852812

Van Dijk, T. A. (1997). What is political discourse analysis? *Belgian Journal of Linguistics*, *11*(1), 11–52.

Waisbord, S. (2018). Why populism and troubling for democratic communication. *Communication, Culture and Critique*, *11*(1), 21–34.

Wittgenstein, L. (2010). *Philosophical investigations*. John Wiley & Sons.

Young, I. M. (1996). Communication and the other: Beyond deliberative democracy. In S. Benhabib (Ed.), *Democracy and difference: Contesting the boundaries of the political* (pp. 120–135). Princeton University Press.

Young, I. M. (1997). Difference as a Resource for democratic communication. In J. Bohman & W. Rehg (Eds.), *Deliberative democracy: Essays on reason and politics* (pp. 383–404). MIT Press. https://ebookcentral-proquest-com.ezproxy.library.uq.edu.au

Zitser, J. (2021, October 10). Donald Trump signals at Iowa rally that he intends to run in 2024, teases that his campaign slogan will be 'Make America Great Again, Again'. *Business Insider*. https://www.businessinsider.com.au/iowa-rally-donald-trump-signals-2024-run-teases-new-slogan-2021-10

Index

Aalberg, T. 47
absolute democratic confusion 110
absolutism 43; *see also* patriotism
Acosta, Jim 95
ad hominem rhetoric 74, 75, 82, 84, 85, 103
Adorno, T. W. 62, 122
adversarial language 49–50
aggression: campaign 85; discursive 99; mediatized 85; verbal 36
algorithmic governmentality 9
Allard, G. 115
Almond, G. 54
Aló Presidente 93, 94
Álvarez, A. 82, 121
"Amor en tiempos de Trump" 86
antagonistic/antagonism 42, 92; discourse 89
Anthony, B. 2
antidemocratic/antidemocracy 1, 2, 51, 81–83, 103, 111
antidialogic/monologic styles 1, 2, 6, 14, 54; political communication 1
appeal 2, 4, 46, 49, 50, 52, 70, 74
Archibugi, D. 9
Arditi, B. 32
Arendt, H. 25, 57
Aristotle 92
Armen Graham, B. 86
arrogance of ignorance 33
audience populism 47–49
Austin, J. L. 34
authoritarian populist actors 3; *see also* populist actors
authoritarian populist communication 42–45, 68; audience populism,

hate speech and cancel culture 47–48; communicative, mediatic and audience dimensions 45–47; populist communication style 49–51; populist media 49; *see also* communicative/communication
authoritarian populist leaders 15, 44, 45
autocracy 6, 14, 61, 100

Babel 10, 11; as metaphor 10–11
Babel 2001 (Meireles' installation) 11
Babelian myth 10, 11
Baily, Jaime 24
Bakhtin, M. M. 1, 10, 34
Ball, T. 9, 11, 120, 121
barbarism 9
Barr, Bill 16
Bennett, W. L. 21
Bickart, B. 93
Biden, Joe 4, 24, 53, 87, 103, 109, 125
"Big Lie" 23, 24, 103
Black Lives Matter protests 8
Blake, A. 102
Block, E. 49, 51, 75, 90
Blumler, J. 34
Bolívar, A. 34, 36, 81, 84, 120, 123
Bolivarian militia 112
Bolivarian socialism 25
Bolivarian Socialism, 21st Century 82
Bolivarian sovereign 88
Bouvier, G. 48
Bracciale, R. 7
Bracho-Polanco, E. 93

Brants, K. 11, 21, 30
Bump, P. 87
Bush, George W. 84

Cabrera, Saul 32
cancel culture 47–48
Cañizález, A. 95
Canovan, M. 32
Capitol 24, 113
Capitol Hill: insurrection 5, 8, 16;
  siege 24; uprising 15
Carroll, R. 71, 97
Cassidy, J. 124
Castro, Fidel 25
centre ground individuals 83
Chávez, Hugo 4, 5, 7, 8, 14–16,
  23–26, 28, 31, 32, 34, 35, 42, 52, 60,
  68, 69–72, 74, 76, 78, 79, 81–103,
  109–111, 113–116, 120–125; *see also*
  individual entries
Chávez-Trump déjà vu: pilot study
  69–72
Chavismo 15
Chenoweth, E. 117
Christopher, T. 101, 102
Chumaceiro, I. 82, 121
Cildo Meireles' installation 11
civic-ness 54
civil leadership 5
Cohen, J. 5, 61
Cold War 5
Comey, James 112
communicative/communication 1,
  2, 7, 9, 10, 14, 22, 23, 33, 35, 36, 53,
  54, 69, 72; commons 122; democracy 13, 14, 51, 57, 62, 111, 122; disruption 2; entropy 11; power 1–2,
  58; style 5, 47; styles 47, 54, 62, 72,
  75; *see also individual entries*
computational capitalism 5
Consejo Nacional Electoral (CNE) 32
contemporary authoritarian populists 123
conventional democracy 13; *see also*
  democratic/democracy
Cooper, Anderson 24
Coordinadora Democratica 113
Cordisco, A. 121
critical political communication 34–36; *see also* political
  communication

cultural backlash thesis 60
cultural imaginaries 44

Davis, A. 5
Deacon, D. 68
de la Torre, C. 33, 122
"Democracy disrupted?" 6
Democracy in Retreat 27
"Democracy in Retreat" 5–6
democratic/democracy 6, 13, 14,
  16, 21–36, 51, 53–56, 60, 62, 110;
  conventions 35, 98; discourses 3, 5,
  6, 13, 33, 53, 55, 62, 68, 69, 72, 78,
  79; discursive and communicative
  13–14, 62; and discursive disruption 2–7, 9–11, 13–17; disrupted
  impressions of 6–7; disruptions 3,
  9, 16, 54, 60, 77; elections 31, 98,
  123; eroded discourses of 26–32;
  erosion 28, 68; freedoms 55, 75, 81;
  key studies, review 27–32; political
  communication 36, 51; politics 9,
  56; populism *vs.* 32–34; societies 7,
  9, 58; values 111; *see also individual*
  entries
Democrats 30, 92, 109
descamisados 52
de Tocqueville, A. 55
de Waal, S. 5
digital disruption 5, 9, 61
discourse as dialogue 36
discursive disruption framework
  1–3, 5, 7, 14, 16, 17, 42, 60–62,
  68–79, 109, 120; analysis and
  method, approach 72–74; analytical framework 73–79, 81; Chávez
  and Trump, paradigms 81–103;
  Chávez-Trump déjà vu 69–72;
  emotionalization of politics 74;
  fear and persuasion 74; frame 3,
  61; implications of 79, 109, 119,
  120; indicators of 79
discursive violence 16, 34–36, 42–62,
  116; as populism 36, 120
disrupted democracy 16, 42–62,
  103, 110; *see also* democratic/
  democracy
disrupted impressions, democracy
  6–7
disrupted public spheres 21
disruption, is discursive 1–17

distorted media reality 31
distrust 15, 29, 83, 113–115
Dryzek, J. 13, 62

Economist Intelligence Unit (EIU)
    26
Edelman 22, 29
Edelman Trust Barometer 26
Edelman Trust Barometer report 29
Edelman Trust Barometer Press
    Release 29
Eisen, N. 6
"*el caudillo yanqui*" 45
electoral processes 116
emotional bond 34, 82
emotions 2, 43, 49–50, 73, 74, 121
Ernst, N. 7, 43, 47
Escalante-Block, E. 43, 74
Escudero, A. 81
ethical language 11
ethnography of communication 69,
    76
exclusion, patterns 21

Fairclough, N. 36
FairVote 100
Farrelly, M. 13, 51
Fernandez, C. 124
Fisher, D. R. 117
Fitzduff, M. 2
flawed democracies 27, 28; *see also*
    democratic/democracy
Fletcher, R. 4
Foucault, M. 36, 55
fourth state 57
four-variable discursive disruption
    frame 79
fragile democracies 45; *see also*
    democratic/democracy
Freedom House 5, 26–27, 95, 98, 103
Freire, P. 1, 34
French, J. R. P. 5
French Revolution 52, 56
Fromm, E. 2
Fukuyama, F. 5, 8
full democracies 27, 28; *see also*
    democratic/democracy

Gamson, W. A. 22
Genesis, book 10
Gill, T. 71

Gillespie, Ed 112
global democracy 26–29; *see also*
    democratic/democracy;
    Economist Intelligence Unit
    (EIU)
global protests 5
Global State of Democracy 28
Globovision 96
Goffman, E. 6
González, A. 116
Gramsci, A. 22, 25
The Guardian 3, 4, 9, 49, 86

Habermas, J. 53
Hameleers, M. 4, 47
Hanson, R. L. 13, 56
Hariman, R. 35
Harper's Magazine 48
hate speech 31, 47–48
Hawkins, K. 3, 4
Heinrich, J. 73
Hepp, A. 1
Herbst, S. 121
The Heritage Foundation 26
Hiebert, T. 10
Higgins, A. 96
Hill-Harris Poll 97
Hitler, A. 23
Hobbes, T. 61
Hofstadter, R. 35
human interaction 22
Human Rights Watch 26, 95,
    98–100, 102, 116
Hymes, D. 68, 69, 72, 76, 77
"hyper-mediatic" leadership 93

identity 61; construction of 88–92;
    disruption 61; politics 8, 14, 15, 47,
    49–51, 86, 88, 89, 91, 110, 116
identity strategized (or weaponized)
    47
"ideological fight" 96
imaginaries 23–26, 32, 52, 89, 121
impoliteness 36, 81, 92, 115, 121,
    123
indicators of discursive disruption
    79, 118
inflammatory language 15
information bankruptcy 29
Inglehart, R. F. 32, 33, 43, 60, 90
insult politics 85

Inter-American Commission of
Human Rights (IACHR) 98, 99
Inter-American Press Association 96

Jagers, J. 47
Jakobson, Roman 36
Jamieson, K. H. 84
Jarvis, Jeff 93
Jong-un, Kim 87
Jon Stewart Show 30
justice 16, 48, 54–56, 99, 100

Katyal, N. 16
Kaul de Marlangeon, S. 121
Kavanaugh, Brett 101
Kayam, O. 43
Khrushchev, Nikita 96
Klein, E. 8
Kopan, T. 85
Krastev, I. 5
Kriesi, H. 47, 57

Laclau, E. 60, 61
Lakoff, G. 93
language: games 120, 121; use 81–88;
see also individual entries
Latin American caudillos 3
Latouche, M. A. 31
Leahy, Patrick 118
legacy media 29, 68, 112, 121, 122
legitimacy 22, 23, 25, 60, 110
Leonardi, R. 22
Levitsky, S. 44–45
Lewandowsky, Stephan 93
liberty 55
lies 21–36; in politics 22–26
Limited Inc 10
Little, Alan 58
logical fallacies 73
"Love in Times of Trump" 86
Loxton, J. 44, 45
Lugo-Ocando, J. 95

Mackaoui, Sean 7
Maingon, T. 99
"Make America First" 25
"Make America Great Again"
(MAGA) 43, 88, 92
Martin, J. 73
mass media 50, 57

Mazzoleni, G. 7, 50
McNamara, Robert 25
media 7, 9, 28–30, 45, 49, 51, 58, 74,
92–97, 103, 122–124; coverage 77;
elites 24, 30; outlets 49, 94, 123;
platforms 31, 57, 59, 74; populism
49; use 50–51; use and relationship
92–97
media Caesarism 95
mediatization 59, 95; of politics 21
Mein Kampf 23
Mercieca, J. 115
metadiscourse 77
middle-ground politics 3; *see also*
centre ground individuals
Miller, Steven 101
Minima Moralia 122
mistrust 9, 29, 30, 32
modern democracy 13, 21; *see also*
democratic/democracy; Western
democracy; Western democratic
discourses
Mogelson, L. 24
moral appeal 8
moral language, populist communication 16, 17, 109–125; Chávez and
Trump 120–125
moral political language 121
Mounk, Y. 15
Muller Probe 112

Nanetti, R 22
Negrine, R. 33, 35, 49, 51, 75
news media 27, 30, 36, 49, 52, 57, 71,
75, 77, 90, 94, 95; coverage 68, 69,
76, 78, 79
The New York Times 85, 101
nonpopulists/nonpopulism 110, 111,
121
Norris, P. 32, 33, 43, 44, 48, 60,
90

Obama, Barrack 58
online news 4
opposition 28, 31, 32, 87, 88, 94, 95,
98, 99, 114, 116, 117

Palacio Martin, J. 59, 110
Papacharissi, Z. 50, 54
Papathanassopoulos, S. 35

"participative" democracy 109; *see also* democratic/democracy
Pateman, C. 54
patriotism 86
Paul, John II (Pope) 24
Pensamiento y Acción 25
Pérez Jiménez, Marcos 112
permanent revolution 25
Peron, Juan Domingo 45
Pew Research Centre 27, 30, 31, 44
Pfetsch, B. 21, 35
Pimentel, O. 116
Pino-Iturrieta, E. 44
polarized political communication 4
political actors 15, 22, 34–36, 47, 124
political communication 10, 21, 30; scholarship 7; shutdowns 14–16, 48; styles 2, 4, 36, 47, 51, 110; *see also individual entries*
political discourse 34–36, 58, 120
political economy developments 15
political language 9, 11, 23, 72
political philosophy 9
political speech 3, 36, 77
politics 73; trust, truths, and lies in 22–26; *see also individual politics*
populism 3–4, 7, 30, 32, 33, 42, 43, 45, 47, 49, 51, 60, 121, 122; democracy *vs.* 32–34; for dummies 45
"Populism for Dummies" *46*
populist actors 4, 35, 75, 123
populist audiences 4, 43, 47, 49, 52, 82, 84, 110, 119, 120
populist caudillos 23
populist communication 4–5, 7, 16, 17, 33–36, 42–62, 79, 120; authoritarian 42–45; moral language of 109–125; research 4; style 33, 35, 36, 49; *see also* communicative/communication
populist communicators 35, 42, 43, 79
populist discourses 7, 52, 88
populist imaginaries 36
populist leaders 4, 6, 7, 34, 35, 43, 46, 47, 50–52, 73, 111, 122, 125
populist media 49
populist players 6, 15, 30, 45, 49–51, 54, 61, 74, 82
populist politicians 2, 50

populist power 110, 111, 121, 122; autocratic, divisive and intolerant language 111–113; Chávez's and Trump's roles 113–116; discursive ethos of 110–120; unrest, protests, physical and discursive violence 116–120
populist rhetoric 3–6, 42
populist speech performances 62, 68, 73
populist style 16, 47, 49, 87
Postill, J. 49
power 1, 2, 4, 6, 7, 22, 33, 53, 54, 59, 72, 92, 98–101, 111, 116, 123, 124; relations/relationships 8, 21, 34–35, 53, 88
Preece, S. 61
presidential power 97, 115
Pressman, J. 117
public sphere 53
Putin, Vladimir 118
Putnam, R. D. 22

QAnon 24, 86
Quealy, K. 85

Radio Caracas Televisión 96
Ramos Avalos, J. 25
Recall Referendum 114
Rendon, M. 124
Republican Party 112
Republicans 30, 31, 58, 110, 112, 121
retribalization, politics 14
Robbins, M. 123
Romero Rodríguez, L. M. 84
Römer Pieretti, M. 84, 89
Roosevelt, Eleanor 26
Rosenberg, P. 93
Rude Democracy 121
Rupar, A. 16

Sanabria, Eduardo (EDO Ilustrado), xvi, 45, 46
Sartori, G. 74, 111
Savage, C. 101
"Save America" speech 115
Schmidt, E. 5, 61
Sclafani, J. 77
Sieyès, Abbé 52
Sillito, D. 93

Silverstein, M. 35, 47
socialist populism 83
social media platforms 6, 21, 31, 45, 48, 51, 57, 58, 102
sovereignty 52, 56, 84
speech acts 9, 49, 62, 76, 78, 82
speech events 73, 76
speech situations 76
speech strategies 81
speech styles 1
speech "taxonomy" 72
Stiegler, B. 5, 9
Stout, D. 84
strategic weapon 121
style 1, 2, 4, 5, 7, 21–36, 47, 49, 51, 85
Suk, J. 101
Suprani, Rayma xiv, 86
Swart, J. 59

Taussig, D. 84
Taylor, C. 23
Tharoor, I. 45
Thiers, C. 115
"Third Estate" 52
Thomas, G. 75
Thompson, M. 9
Thunberg, Greta 10
Tilley, C. 93
totality 62
traditional democratic discourses 97–103
Trump, Donald 2–7, 15, 16, 23–26, 31, 35, 42, 45, 52–53, 59, 68–72, 74, 76, 78, 79, 81–103, 109–111, 113, 115–118, 120–125; *see also individual entries*
trust 21–36, 110; in politics 22–26; sociology approach 22
truths 21–36; in politics 22–26

United Nations Human Rights 14

Vaccari, C. 51
Valeriani, A. 51
Van Aelst, P. 33
Van Dijk, T. A. 36
variables 49, 52, 62, 68, 75–79, 81, 97; of discursive disruption 75–76, 79, 81
Verba, S. 54
verbal aggression 36; *see also* aggression
verbal violence 116; *see also* discursive violence
Viroli, M. 55
vivere politico 55
Vollmer, H. 5, 34
Voltmer, K. 11, 21
Von Vacano, D. 45

Waisbord, S. 21, 122
Walgrave, S. 47
The Washington Post 15, 45, 87, 102
Wehner, L. E. 115
Welsch, F. F. 44, 99
Western democracy 62
Western democratic discourses 51–52, 55–57; discursive and communicative approach 52–54; shrinking common ground 57–59
Wheeler, Ted 58
Williams, R. 43
Winberg, O. 85
Wittgenstein, L. 120
Wittmeyer, A. P. Q. 82
Wodak, R. 33, 36

Young, I. M. 13, 14, 23, 51, 54, 56, 62, 88, 111, 122